TABLE OF CONTENTS

ACRONYMS

AAA	Anti-Aircraft Artillery
ACU	Army Combat Uniform
ADRP	Army Doctrinal Reference Publication
ANA	Afghan National Army
ANZUS	Australia, New Zealand, United States Security Treaty
AO	Area of Operations
AOR	Area of Responsibility
APC	Armored Personnel Carrier
AQ	al-Qaeda
AR	Army Regulation
BDU	Battle Dress Uniform
BFV	Bradley Fighting Vehicle
BOG	Boots on the Ground
CA	Civil Affairs
CAAT	Combined Arms Assessment Team
CALL	Center for Army Lessons Learned
CAS	Close Air Support
CCA	Close Combat Attack
CFC-A	Combined Forces Command - Afghanistan
CINCCENT	Commander, Central Command
CINCLANT	Commander, Atlantic Command
CJCS	Chairman of the Joint Chiefs of Staff
CJTF	Combined Joint Task Force
CMH	Center of Military History
COIN	Counterinsurgency
COP	Combat Outpost

CPF	Caribbean Peacekeeping Forces
CSAR	Combat Search and Rescue
DACOWITS	U.S. Department of Defense Advisory Committee on Women in the Service
DCU	Desert Camouflage Uniform
DOD	Department of Defense
EA	Eastern Alliance
ETP	Exception to Policy
FLOT	Forward Line of Own Troops
FM	Field Manual
FMC	Fully Mission Capable
FOB	Forward Operating Base
FY	Fiscal Year
GCC	Ground Component Command
GDI	Ground-Directed Interdiction
GPS	Global Positioning System
GWOT	Global War on Terror
HMMWV	High Mobility Multipurpose Wheeled Vehicle
IED	Improvised Explosive Device
IRGC	Iraqi Republican Guard Corps
JCS	Joint Chiefs of Staff
JEWEL	Joint Effort for Welfare, Education, and Liberation
JFC-N	Joint Forces Command-North
JFC-E	Joint Forces Command-East
JTF	Joint Task Force
KFIA	King Fahd International Airport
KFOR	Kosovo Force
KIA	Killed in Action

KTO	Kuwaiti Theater of Operations
LAV	Light Armored Vehicle
LBE	Load Bearing Equipment
LCM	Landing Craft, Mechanized
LOC	Line of Communication
MARCENT	Marine Central Command
MLRS	Multiple-Launch Rocket System
MOS	Military Occupational Specialties
MRE	Meal, Ready-to-Eat
NA	Northern Alliance
NATO	North Atlantic Treaty Organization
NCEAS	National Center for Ecological Analysis and Synthesis
NDAA	National Defense Authorization Act
OAS	Organization of American States
ODA	Operational Detachment-Alpha
OECS	Organization of Eastern Caribbean States
OEF	Operation Enduring Freedom
OPORD	Operations Order
OPLAN	Operation Plan
POW	Prisoner of War
PRT	Provincial Reconstruction Team
PX	Post Exchange
ROE	Rules of Engagement
RPG	Rocket Propelled Grenade
RSOI	Reception, Staging, and Onward Integration
SEAD	Suppression of Enemy Air Defenses
SOF	Special Operations Forces

TAA	Tactical Assembly Area
TF	Task Force
TOW	Tube-launched, Optical-tracked, Wire-guided
UBL	Usama bin Ladin
UN	United Nations
UNMOVIC	United Nations Monitoring, Verification, and Inspection Commission
UNSCR	United Nations Security Council Resolution
USARCENT	U.S. Army Central (Third U.S. Army)
USF	U.S. Forces
USCENTCOM	United States Army Central Command
USLANTCOM	United States Army Atlantic Command
WIA	Wounded in Action

TABLES

INTRODUCTION

On January 9, 2013, Chairman of the Joint Chiefs of Staff (CJCS) General Martin E. Dempsey informed Secretary of Defense Leon Panetta of his intent to "rescind the direct combat exclusion rule for women and to eliminate all unnecessary gender-based barriers to [military] service."[1] In the same informational memorandum, Dempsey outlined a multi-year plan to validate soldier physical and occupational standards, assess the operational impact of complete gender integration, and ultimately "integrate women into the remaining restricted occupational fields within our military."[2] The proposed reversal of this longstanding female assignment policy immediately ignited debate within the U.S. Army over the potential impact of complete gender-integration. Many of these discussions centered on the continued validity of the evidence used to support the U.S. Army's 1992 policy excluding female soldiers from service in direct ground combat units.[3] The importance of this issue demands more than a return to decades old data, however; it calls for a complete reevaluation of the logical underpinning of the U.S. Army's original combat exclusion policy. What follows is a comparison of the assumptions made by the Presidential Commission on the Assignment of Women in the Armed Forces regarding the conditions and requirements of combat to the realities of war as experienced and reported by soldiers over the last three decades. This analysis enables an examination of the validity of the U.S. Army's original combat exclusion policy and illuminates the level of operational risk associated with its revocation.

---

[1] Martin E. Dempsey, "Women in the Service Implementation Plan," Memorandum for Secretary of Defense (Washington D.C., January 9, 2013).

[2] Dempsey, "Women in the Service Implementation Plan."

[3] Kathleen Curthoys, "Readers Question Putting Women In Combat," *Army Times*, (February 4, 2012).

Background

Polices governing the assignment of female service members have instigated intense social and political debate since the official inclusion of women in the military in 1948.[4] Current dialogue often centers on the existing Department of Defense (DOD) policy excluding women from service with direct ground combat units. The inception of this policy dates back to 1988, when the DOD Task Force on Women in the Military acknowledged discrepancies in the understanding and application of the combat exclusion policy among the Services. The matter became a point of legislative contention three years later, in 1991, during congressional debate over the National Defense Authorization Act (NDAA) for Fiscal Years (FY) 1992 and 1993.[5] As a result of this increased congressional concern, when the final version of the bill passed in December 1991 it included provisions for a Presidential Commission on the Assignment of Women in the Armed Forces (hereafter referred to as the Presidential Commission). Through the NDAA FY 92-93, Congress charged the Presidential Commission to evaluate the legal and doctrinal framework surrounding the assignment of female service members and provide recommendations on "what roles servicewomen should have in combat" to the President no later than December 1992.[6]

After conducting an extensive study, the Presidential Commission recommended the continued exclusion of women from positions within direct ground combat units on the premise that female service members were unsuited to the unique requirements of these assignments.

---

[4] Women's Armed Services Integration Act of 1948, Public Law 80-625, U.S. Statutes at Large 62 (1948).

[5] U.S. Department of Defense Task Force on Women in the Military, *Report* (Washington D.C.: Department of Defense, 1988), 15.

[6] United States, Presidential Commission on the Assignment of Women in the Armed Forces, *Report to the President* (Washington D.C.: The Commission, 1992), iii-iv.

Specifically, the Presidential Commission highlighted the necessity of soldiers in direct ground combat units to perform their duties in conditions requiring extreme physical exertion in austere environments under the constant risk of injury, capture, or death.[7] In support of this recommendation, the Presidential Commission cited research detailing the physiological differences between male and female soldiers and the predicted psychological impact of female soldiers on unit cohesion.[8]

The U.S. Army also codified its prohibition on the assignment of female soldiers to units engaged in direct combat or collocated with units engaged in direct combat in 1992 with the publication of Army Regulation (AR) 600-13, *Army Policy for the Assignment of Female Soldiers*.[9] Since its publication, the U.S. Army has amended this policy only once. In June 2012, in response to requirements levied by Congress and the DOD, Secretary of the Army John McHugh reviewed AR 600-13 and rescinded all items prohibiting the assignment of female soldiers to units doctrinally required to collocate with direct ground combat units.[10] Despite this important alteration, AR 600-13 continues to preclude the assignment of female soldiers to

---

[7] Presidential Commission, *Report to the President*, 24.

[8] Presidential Commission, *Report to the President*, 24-27 and C-1 – C-139. Significantly, the Presidential Commission readily admits, "there are *no* authoritative military studies of mixed-gender ground combat cohesion." (25, emphasis added) The Presidential Commission goes on to clarify that their concerns are for "the effects that women *could* have on the cohesion of ground combat units," characterizing these effects as "*unknown* but *probably* negative." (25 and 27, emphasis added).

[9] U.S. Department of the Army, Army Regulation 600-13, *Army Policy for the Assignment of Female Soldiers* (Washington D.C.: U.S. Department of the Army, March 27, 1992), 1.

[10] For information on the official Congressional and DOD mandates regarding the review of female soldier assignment policies, see: Ike Skelton National Defense Authorization Act for Fiscal Year 2011, Public Law 111-383, 111th Cong., 2d sess. (January 7, 2011), § 535; "Department Opens More Military Positions to Women," Department of Defense press release, U.S. Department of Defense Office of the Assistant Secretary of Defense (Public Affairs), http://www.defense.gov/Releases/Release.aspx?ReleaseID=15051 (accessed January 28, 2013).

positions and units with the "primary mission to engage in direct combat on the ground."[11] Consequently, eighteen U.S. Army Military Occupational Specialties (MOS) remain closed to female soldiers.[12]

However, on January 9, 2013 the DOD announced its intent to remove these final barriers to the complete gender integration of the military. Specifically, CJCS General Martin E. Dempsey ordered all Services to immediately expand and enforce all existing exceptions to the combat exclusion policy, develop gender-neutral occupational standards for use in assessing and assigning all service members no later than September 2015, and assess the operational impact of complete gender integration by the first quarter of FY 2016.[13] The following analysis complements these efforts by examining the degree of correlation between the combat conditions assumed by the Presidential Commission and the actual conditions reported by soldiers participating in U.S. Army campaigns over the last thirty years in order to determine the amount of operational risk associated with rescinding the combat exclusion policy.[14]

---

[11] John McHugh, "Army Directive 2012-16 (Changes to Army Policy for the Assignment of Female Soldiers)," Memorandum For Commanders, U.S. Army Major Commands (Washington D.C., May 7, 2012), 2.

[12] U.S. Department of the Army, Department of the Army Pamphlet 611-21, *Military Occupational Classification and Structures* (Washington, D.C.: U.S. Department of the Army, January 22, 2007), Table 13-1.

[13] Dempsey, "Women in the Service Implementation Plan."

[14] Within the U.S. Army there are no official or commonly accepted definitions of operational risk. However, by applying the concept of risk to the operational level of war, the following composite definition emerges: operational risk is the probability and severity of loss, linked to hazards encountered during campaigns and major operations, which impact the achievement of strategic objectives within theaters or other operational areas. For the definitions of risk and operational level of war, see U.S. Department of the Army, Field Manual (FM) 5-19, *Composite Risk Management* (Washington, D.C.: U.S. Department of the Army, August 2006), Glossary-7; U.S. Department of Defense, Joint Publication 1-02, *Department of Defense Dictionary of Military and Associated Terms* (Washington, D.C.: Headquarters, U.S. Department of Defense, August 15, 2011), 254.

<u>Thesis</u>

The first concern listed by the Presidential Commission, the negative psychological impact of women on unit cohesion, remains unproven.[15] As a result, it is not a valid criterion for the continued exclusion of female soldiers from ground combat units and is omitted from the remainder of this study. Evidence supporting the second concern, the physiological limitations of female soldiers, is accepted as accurate and not disputed.[16] However, historical analysis of the

---

[15] For further discussion regarding the lack of empirical evidence supporting the causal relationship of women to reduced military unit cohesion, see Presidential Commission, *Report to the President*, 24-27, C-80 – C-82; Margaret C. Harrell and Laura L. Miller, *New Opportunities for Military Women: Effects Upon Readiness, Cohesion, and Morale* (Santa Monica, CA: Rand, 1997); Laurie M. Porter and Rick V. Adside, "Women in Combat: Attitudes and Experiences of U.S. Military Officers and Enlisted Personnel" (master's thesis, Naval Postgraduate School, 2001); Robert J. MacCoun, Elizabeth Kier and Aaron Belkin, "Does Social Cohesion Determine Motivation in Combat?: An Old Question with an Old Answer," *Armed Forces and Society* 32, no. 4 (July 2006): 646-654; U.S. Defense Department Advisory Committee on Women in the Services (DACOWITS), *2009 Report*, by Claudia J. Kennedy, Roberta L. Santiago, and Felipe Torres (Washington D.C.: U.S. Department of Defense, 2010), 13. For dissenting opinion on the impact of women on military unit cohesion, see Kathleen F. Kirk, "Women in Combat?" (report presented to the Faculty of the School of Education in partial fulfillment of the Requirements for the course Education 795 A&B Seminar, San Diego State University, 1988); Leonard Wong, Thomas A. Kolditz, Raymond A. Millen, and Terrence M. Potter, "Why They Fight: Combat Motivation in War" (monograph, U.S. Army War College, 2003); Leora N. Rosen, Kathryn H. Knudson, and Peggy Fancher, "Cohesion and the Culture of Hypermasculinity in U.S. Army Units," *Armed Forces and Society* 29, no. 3 (Spring 2003): 325-351; Kingsley Brown, *Co-Ed Combat: The New Evidence That Women Shouldn't Fight the Nation's Wars* (New York: Penguin, 2007), 127-229.

[16] Presidential Commission, *Report to the President*, 24-27 and C-1 – C-139. For research replicating these original findings in the two decades since the original publication of the *Report to the President,* see William Gregor, "Why Can't Anything Be Done? Measuring Physical Readiness of Women for Military Occupations" (paper presented at the 2011 International Biennial Conference of the Inter-University Seminar on Armed Forces and Society, Chicago, IL, October 21-23, 2011). For research demonstrating that physical task performance by female soldiers can be improved through targeted training programs, see: Everett Harman, Peter Frykman, Christopher Palmer, Eric Lammi, Katy Reynolds, and Verne Backus, "Effects of a Specifically Designed Physical Conditioning Program on the Load Carriage and Lifting Performance of Female Soldiers" (technical report, U.S. Army Research of Environmental Medicine, November 1997); William P. Ebben and Randall L. Jensen, "Strength Training for Women: Debunking the Myths That Block Opportunity," *The Physician and Sportsmedicine* 26, no. 5 (May 1998): 2; Adam N. Wojack, "Integrating Women Into the Infantry," *Military Review* 82 (November-December 2002): 67-74.

5

campaigns executed by the U.S. Army over the past thirty years indicates that while the

Presidential Commission's concerns regarding the hazards and demands of war remain valid, they

are significantly mitigated by advances in the technology and doctrine used by the U.S. Army. As

a result, the revocation of the combat exclusion policy poses a low operational risk to the U.S.

Army.[17]

Methodology

Official military histories, published soldier memoirs and interviews, and Center for

Army Lessons Learned (CALL) reports provide the main sources of data used in the following

analysis. These documents establish a clear understanding of the nature of the environment and

operations experienced by soldiers deployed in support of U.S. Army campaigns conducted

between 1982-2012. According to former Secretaries of Defense Donald Rumsfeld and Robert

Gates, the combat experiences of this period provide the best approximation of the military

conflicts America will face in the future and thus offer a temporal boundary for this study.[18] To

ensure the relevance of the analysis to service in direct combat conditions, this study includes

only those campaigns awarded a campaign ribbon for display on the Army flag staff by the U.S.

Army Center of Military History (CMH). The names, locations, and dates of these campaigns are

listed in Table 1, where they have also been categorized by type of operation.

Table 1. U.S. Army Campaigns, 1982-2012

Campaign	Location	Date	Type of Operation

---

[17] For specific information regarding the U.S. Army's process for assessing the probability and severity of risk, see U.S. Department of the Army, FM 5-19, 1-10.

[18] Donald H. Rumsfeld, *Quadrennial Defense Review* (Washington, D.C.: U.S. Department of Defense, February 2006), vi-vii, 75; Robert M. Gates, *Quadrennial Defense Review* (Washington, D.C.: U.S. Department of Defense, February 2010), v-vi.

Urgent Fury	Grenada	October 25 – November 21, 1983	Limited Contingency
Just Cause	Panama	December 20, 1989 – January 31, 1990	Limited Contingency
Desert Shield and Desert Storm	Saudi Arabia and Kuwait	1990-1991	Large-Scale Combat
Allied Force and Joint Guardian	Kosovo	1999-present	Peacekeeping
Enduring Freedom	Afghanistan	2001-present	Counterinsurgency
Iraqi Freedom	Iraq	2003-2012	Counterinsurgency

Source: U.S. Army Center of Military History; U.S. Department of the Army, Army Doctrinal Reference Publication (ADRP) 3-0, Unified Land Operations; U.S. Department of Defense, Joint Publication 1, Doctrine for the Armed Forces of the United States.

In order to eliminate redundant evidence, this study includes only one representation of each type of military operation conducted during this time period. As Operations Urgent Fury and Enduring Freedom occurred nearest to the chronological beginning and end dates of the time period studied and thus allow for the broadest base of analysis, they have been selected over Operations Just Cause and Iraqi Freedom to represent limited contingency and counterinsurgency operations, respectively.[19]

The contextual information gleaned via case study analysis provides the means to evaluate this data set. This process enables a comparison the actual conditions reported during these campaigns to the assumptions regarding combat made by the Presidential Commission, specifically: the frequency and types of missions performed by units, the equipment issued and

---

[19] U.S. Army Center of Military History (CMH), "Campaigns of the U.S. Army," U.S. Army CMH, http://www.history.army.mil/html/reference/campaigns.html (accessed October 3, 2012); U.S. Department of the Army, Army Doctrinal Reference Publication (ADRP) 3-0, *Unified Land Operations* (Washington D.C.: Headquarters, U.S. Department of the Army, May 2012), 1-6; U.S. Department of Defense, Joint Publication 1, *Doctrine for the Armed Forces of the United States* (Washington D.C.: U.S. Department of Defense, March 25, 2013), I-14.

used during operations, soldier living conditions, casualty rates, and prisoner of war (POW)

capture rates and behaviors.[20] Synthesis of these comparisons facilitates a determination of

operational risk in accordance with the parameters established in U.S. Army Field Manual 5-19,

Composite Risk Management.

CASE STUDIES

Operation Urgent Fury, Grenada

The roots of American military intervention in Grenada in 1983, code-named Operation

Urgent Fury, directly emanated from the illegitimate rise to power of the left-leaning New Joint

Effort for Welfare, Education, and Liberation (JEWEL) movement. Originally helmed by

Maurice Bishop, New JEWEL overthrew the democratically elected government of Sir Eric Gairy

in 1979 and "immediately signed trade and military agreements" with the governments of Cuba

and Russia.[21] Though noticeably lopsided, these relationships benefited both the fledgling

Grenadian government and the Communist Bloc. Specifically, Cuba gained control over key

American air and sea lines of communication (LOC) through the Antilles in return for subsidizing

the construction of a military-grade aerial runway in the Grenadian hamlet of Point Salines.[22]

---

[20] Presidential Commission, *Report to the President*, 24-25.

[21] Richard W. Stewart, *Operation Urgent Fury: The Invasion of Grenada, October 1983* (Washington D.C.: Center of Military History, 2008), 7; "International," *New York Times*, November 5, 1983; "International," *New York Times*, November 6, 1983; Susan Tifft, Johanna McGeary and Christopher Redman, "A Treasure Trove of Documents," *Time* 122, no. 21 (1983): 44; United States Department of State and Department of Defense, *Grenada: A Preliminary Report* (Washington D.C.: Government Printing Office, 1983), 18-30.

[22] National Center for Ecological Analysis and Synthesis (NCEAS), "Commercial Activity (Shipping)," NCEAS, http://www.nceas.ucsb.edu/globalmarine/impacts (accessed November 26, 2012); Ronald H. Cole, *Operation URGENT FURY: The Planning and Execution of Joint Operations in Grenada 12 October-2 November 1983* (Washington D.C.: Joint History Office, Office of the Chairman of the Joint Chiefs of Staff, 1997), 9; Ronald Reagan, "Address to the Nation on Defense and National Security," March 23, 1983, in *Public Papers of the Presidents of the United States: Ronald Reagan, 1983*, vol 1 (Washington, D.C.: United States

These developments signaled unprecedented Communist encroachment in the western

hemisphere. Within the context of the Cold War, such a power play greatly concerned the small

island nations of the Caribbean. Consequently, in 1981 they formed the Organization of Eastern

Caribbean States (OECS) in an attempt to protect the sovereignty and stability of the region.[23]

However, when political turmoil in Grenada again intensified two years later the OECS publically

abandoned their position of neutrality and welcomed American overtures to provide security

assistance.[24]

On October 12, 1983, the Grenadian crisis began in earnest. Disillusioned with Prime

Minister Bishop's promises of economic progress and assuming the public would support his

decision, Grenadian Deputy Prime Minister, Bernard Coard, assisted by the Commander in Chief

of the Grenadian Armed Forces, General Hudson Austin, assumed control of the government and

placed Bishop under house arrest. A week later, however, the public rallied behind Bishop and

freed him from confinement. The same riotous crowd that freed Bishop then attempted to overrun

the Grenadian Army headquarters at Fort Rupert on Bishop's behalf; however, soldiers loyal to

Coard and Austin fought back. Maneuvering three armored personnel carriers alongside the

crowd, the soldiers opened fire, slaughtering Bishop and at least ten other civilians.[25] As word of

---

Government Printing Office, 1984), 440.

[23] Antigua, Dominica, Grenada, Montserrat, St. Kitts/Nevis, Saint Lucia, and Saint Vincent and the Grenadines, "Treaty Establishing the Organization of Eastern Caribbean States," June 18, 1981, *United Nations Treaty Series: Treaties and International Agreements Registered or Filed and Recorded with the Secretariat of the United Nations* 1338, no. I-22435 (1981): 97.

[24] Ronald Reagan, National Security Decision Directive no. 105, "Eastern Caribbean Regional Security Policy," *Code of Federal Regulations*, Title 3, http://www.fas.org/irp/offdocs/nsdd/nsdd-105.pdf (accessed November 26, 2012); Cole, *Operation URGENT FURY*, 22.

[25] Roberta Morris, "Grenadians Recount Horror of PM's Killing," *Toronto Star*, May 11, 1986; Stewart, *Operation Urgent Fury,* 8; Cole, *Operation URGENT FURY*, 10-11.

the murders spread throughout the country, Austin dissolved Coard's floundering government and installed himself as President of a new Revolutionary Military Council. To instill order, Austin closed the international airport and imposed a strict curfew, warning Grenadians that "violators would be shot on sight."[26]

Bishop's death also prompted a flurry of political and military activity within the United States. Increasingly concerned that the new Grenadian military regime would harm or hold hostage the hundreds of American medical students studying on the island, the Joint Chiefs of Staff sent a warning order to U.S. Atlantic Command (USLANTCOM) on October 20. The order instructed USLANTCOM planners to develop courses of action designed to "protect and evacuate U.S. and designated foreign nationals from Grenada."[27] However, President Reagan did not order planning for military operations to begin until October 22, after the OECS invoked the internal defense clause of their charter and officially requested American assistance.[28] On October 23, USLANTCOM commander (CINCLANT) Admiral Wesley L. McDonald created Joint Task Force (JTF) 120 for the purposes of executing the President's guidance, placing Vice Admiral Joseph Metcalf III at the helm of operation Urgent Fury. McDonald allocated Metcalf one special operations force (SOF) task force (TF), one naval task group, one U.S. Army TF (known as TF

---

[26] Beverly Bowen, "Grenadians are Shocked, Bewildered," *The Globe and Mail*, October 21, 1983; Cole, *Operation URGENT FURY*, 11.

[27] John William Vessey Jr., Msgs, Vessey to CINCLANT, CINCMAC, and CINCRED, 20 0347Z Oct 1983, sub: Warning Order—Grenada NEO, and McDonald to JCS, 20 0616Z Oct 1983, quoted in Edgar F. Raines, Jr., *The Rucksack War: U.S. Army Operational Logistics in Grenada, 1983* (Washington, D.C.: Center of Military History, 2010), 84.

[28] Antigua, et al., "Treaty Establishing the Organization of Eastern Caribbean States," 102-103; Specifically, the OECS charter extends the OECS Defense and Security Committee the power to "advise the [OECS] on matters relating to external defence and on arrangements for collective security against external aggression, *including mercenary aggression, with or without the support of internal of national elements.*" (Emphasis added). See also: Cole, *Operation URGENT FURY*, 22 and 26.

121), and one U.S. Marine Corps TF. On October 24th –having had less than 48-hours notice—

each of these elements arrived at their initial assault position.[29]

Operation Urgent Fury commenced at 0530 hours the following morning, October 25,

1983. CH-46 "Sea Knight" helicopters inserted the marines of the 2nd Battalion, 8th Marine

Regiment (2-8 Marines) "south of Pearls Airport on the east coast of Grenada;" quickly followed

by the airborne assault of 1st Battalion, 75th Ranger Regiment (1-75th) onto the Point Salines

runway.[30] Approximately thirty minutes later, helicopters inserted 12-man SOF teams at four

separate locations:

> the Richmond Hill Prison to rescue political prisoners, the broadcast studio and
> transmitter of Radio Free Grenada to prevent the regime from calling for popular
> resistance to the landings, the headquarters of the People's Revolutionary Army at Fort
> Rupert to disrupt command and control, and the governor general's residence to protect
> Sir Paul Scoon and his family.[31]

Once on the ground, the terrain these units encountered was as diverse as their mission

sets. Near Port Salines, soldiers conducted foot movements of between 500-1000 meters over

terrain that included rolling hills, as well as improved and unimproved roads. Further north,

marines moved similar distances by foot, but over terrain that resembled marshy wetlands. The

intensity of enemy resistance also varied by location. For example, the 1-75th required almost

seven hours to secure Point Salines due to intense enemy anti-aircraft artillery (AAA) and ground

---

[29] For detailed information on the task organization used during Operation Urgent Fury see Raines Jr., *The Rucksack War*, 109. For information regarding deployment timelines, see: Raines, Jr., *The Rucksack War*, 116; Ronald Spector, *U.S. Marines in Grenada, 1983* (Washington, D.C.: headquarters, U.S. Marine Corps History and Museums Division, 1987), 6; "Grenada Chronology" (working paper, Center for Army Lessons Learned, n.d.).

[30] Stewart, *Operation Urgent Fury,* 15; "Grenada Chronology" (working paper, Center for Army Lessons Learned, n.d.); Spector, *U.S. Marines in Grenada*, 6.

[31] Raines, Jr., *The Rucksack War,* 241; Cole, *Operation URGENT FURY,* 41-45.

fire, while the 2-8 Marines secured Pearls Airport in less than two hours after warding off a few half-hearted rounds from retreating Grenadian forces.[32]

However, while the external conditions encountered by these units varied greatly, there was an element of internal consistency in each unit. For example, each soldier met the enemy carrying roughly the same equipment. On average, they carried three-days worth of ammunition, two-days worth of water and rations, "personal issue items (extra pairs of socks, underwear, and spare uniforms), and necessities (toothpaste, hand soap, toilet paper, and razors.)"[33] Additionally, they wore winter-weight battle dress uniforms (BDU), leather boots, Kevlar protective vests and helmets, and carried a weapon.[34] Using the weight of modern military gear as a guide, adjusting upward for the heavier weight of military equipment in 1983, and accounting for individual deviations from the packing list, these soldiers entered the fight carrying a minimum of 85 pounds (lbs.) of gear.[35] Given this preponderance of evidence, there can be no doubt that the initial

---

[32] Terrain assessments made from maps and descriptions in Raines, Jr., *The Rucksack War,* 245 and Spector, *U.S. Marines in Grenada,* 8. Enemy and friendly force activity information can be found in: Raines, Jr., *The Rucksack War,* 245-247; "Invasion in Grenada," *New York Times*, October 28, 1983; "Grenada Chronology" (working paper, Center for Army Lessons Learned, n.d.), 4; Richard W. Stewart, ed. *American Military History Volume II: The United States Army in a Global Era, 1917-2003* (Washington D.C.: Center of Military History, 2005), 395.

[33] For a detailed summary of the packing lists for initial assault forces see Raines Jr., *The Rucksack War,* 176 and 187. Information included here specifically refers to information collected from the 1/75th and 2nd Brigade, 82nd Airborne Infantry Division (2/82), as these elements were on the ground in Grenada within eight hours of the commencement of the invasion. Additionally, for visual representation of packing list information via historical photographs taken during the operation, see Rains, Jr., *The Rucksack War,* 181, 188, 217, 244.

[34] Raines, Jr., *The Rucksack War*, 213; Spector, *U.S. Marines in Grenada,* 8.

[35] Cross-case analysis of all case studies presented in this monograph indicates that during the time period studied, the average U.S. Army soldier carried a period-appropriate version of a standard combat load. For further information, see Appendix B, Equipment Weights and Load Calculations. Specifically with regard to Operation Urgent Fury, additional evidence that this number is likely correct, if not high, was gleaned by Raines, Jr. from interviews conducted with leaders in 3rd Brigade, 82nd Airborne Division (3/82ABN), the unit that followed

assault on Grenada required soldiers to carry heavy equipment while moving relatively short distances on foot, and facing a varied—but constant—enemy threat.

Plagued by logistical failures at the operational level, soldiers deployed to Grenada continued to face similar hardships for the following seventy-two hours. Most notably, the TF 121 commander's decision to deploy additional infantry forces to Grenada before reuniting the operational support and sustainment elements of 1-75th and 2-8 Marines delayed arrival of much-needed vehicles, supplies, and water.[36] Many units compensated for these shortages by confiscating the civilian vehicles and equipment necessary to complete their missions.[37] These expediencies relieved pressure on the logistical units operating in secured areas, however, they reportedly did not lessen the burden on combat units. In particular, JTF 120 stated in an after-action review that the lack of combat vehicles "added to the individual soldiers [sic] load and diminished the fighting capability of the ground force."[38] However, an objective examination of the operations of 2nd and 3rd Battalions, 325th Infantry Regiment (2-325IN and 3-325IN, respectively) does not entirely validate this claim. These units provide a representative sample of

---

2nd Brigade, 82nd Airborne Division (2/82ABN) into Grenada. Reportedly, these elements chose to forgo use of their "A-bag" (a duffle bag usually allotted for a soldier's personal gear and transported separately by their associated sustainment unit) and thus would have likely deployed with heavier rucksacks. However, these officers reported that soldiers' rucksacks "weighed between seventy and eighty pounds when they finished loading them." See Raines, Jr., *The Rucksack War*, 313 for further. For a comprehensive listing of the weight of individual military equipment currently used in combat, see Task Force Devil Combined Arms Assessment Team (CAAT), *The Modern Warrior's Combat Load: Dismounted Operations in Afghanistan, April-May 2003* (Fort Leavenworth: Center for Army Lessons Learned, 2003), 107-111.

[36] Gilbert S. Harper, "Logistics in Grenada: Supporting No-Plan Wars," *Parameters* 20 (June 1990): 58-60; Raines, Jr., *The Rucksack War*, 318, 544; JTF 120, "Grenada After Action Review" (briefing, Center for Army Lessons Learned, n.d.).

[37] Raines, Jr., *The Rucksack War*, 425-426, 456.

[38] JTF 120, "Grenada After-Action Review" (briefing, Center for Army Lessons Learned, n.d.).

units operating on the island from October 26-28; for reference, the experiences of 2-325IN represent the most arduous conditions reported by any unit operating in Grenada during this period, while the operations of 3-325IN represent experiences similar to those recounted by the majority of units on the island.

Having arrived in Grenada on the evening of October 25, 2-325IN and 3-325IN began to maneuver east just after dawn the following morning. As members of TF 121, these units joined the 1-75th in consolidating and expanding the defense of Point Salines. In the far northwest, B Company, 2-325IN (B/2-325IN) engaged in "the most intense close combat for any element of the 82d Airborne Division during URGENT FURY."[39] Ambushed enroute to attack an enemy-held compound north of the village of Calliste, B/2-325IN maneuvered only 800 meters in three and a half hours; ultimately suffering two soldiers killed in action (KIA) and seven soldiers wounded in action (WIA) before declaring their objective secure. On their flank, A Company, 2-325IN (A/2-325IN) pursued a small contingent of enemy soldiers attempting to escape into the jungle ahead of B Company's advance. Despite only traveling an additional 100 meters, the combination of increasingly steep terrain and rapidly mounting temperatures quickly took a toll on the company. Per the A Company commander, the unit suffered so many heat casualties so rapidly that he "almost immediately" instructed his men to "remove their flak jackets and tie them to their rucksacks" before pursuing the enemy soldiers any further.[40] Unaware of the A Company situation, B/2-325 IN completed its post-combat consolidation and re-organization at Calliste and pushed east toward its next objective—the Radio Free Grenada broadcast station south of Grand Anse Beach. Laboring under the weight of their equipment and stifled by the heat and humidity of the jungle, however, the soldiers of B Company quickly suffered the same fate as their peers.

---

[39] Raines, Jr., *The Rucksack War,* 341.

[40] Raines, Jr., *The Rucksack War,* 342.

The company required five hours to travel the one-kilometer distance to the broadcast station, losing thirty soldiers to heat injuries along the way.[41]

Originally held in reserve, C Company, 2-325 IN (C/2-325IN) assumed responsibility for securing the Grenadian military complex at Frequente after the 325 IN battalion commander committed A/2-325IN to the Calliste compound fight. Able to skirt the steep terrain facing A and B Companies in the north, C Company maneuvered easily through 1800 meters of jungle to their objective. The company quickly seized Frequente, belatedly accepting the surrender of the single soldier present at the facility. Following the Frequente mission, C Company – indeed, all of 2-325IN – made contact with only one other enemy force. 2-325IN's final direct combat engagement during Operation Urgent Fury occurred when a Cuban mounted patrol, unaware of the C/2-235IN presence at Frequente, attempted to ambush a 2-325IN reconnaissance element and instead perished in the face of C Company's superior defenses and firepower.[42]

Just south of C/2-325IN, 3-325IN was also pressing east in accordance with the TF 121 operations order (OPORD). Company-sized elements conducted limited attacks to secure key terrain near the town of Ruth Howard and True Blue Point. Also relegated to foot marches, but reaping the benefits of better topography, 3-325IN units easily traveled the one kilometer to their objectives along wide avenues of approach across relatively flat terrain. Throughout the day, they made contact with only a single enemy soldier, a sniper, which American troops killed when he refused to surrender.[43] Though dramatically different from the experiences of 2-325IN, 3-325IN dealt with conditions similar to many other units involved in the operation, such as the marines

---

[41] Raines, Jr., *The Rucksack War,* 340 - 343.

[42] Raines, Jr., *The Rucksack War,* 340-343.

[43] Raines, Jr., *The Rucksack War,* 346.

maneuvering from Pearls and Grenville to St. George.[44] Overall, the experiences of all but one battalion indicate that despite the lack of vehicular support, the majority of combat units maintained swift and unopposed movement because of the nature of the terrain on which they fought and relatively low intensity of the threat.

By October 28, U.S. and Caribbean Peacekeeping Forces (CPF) controlled the island and had begun to transition to the second phase of the operation—pacification. This change in conditions, called "dramatic" by TF 121 Chief of Staff COL Peter J. Boylan, prompted leaders to significantly downgrade uniform standards.[45] Specifically, photographic evidence indicates that soldiers patrolled without rucksacks or Kevlar protective vests, carrying only a day's worth of food and water, their weapon, and basic load of ammunition.[46] Soldier mobility also improved, as the arrival of force sustainment units to the theater finally broke the JTF's logistical logjam and expedited the arrival and distribution of tactical vehicles.[47] Throughout the island, U.S. soldiers executed their assigned pacification missions without incident, prompting the JTF 120 commander to announce the cessation of hostilities and the dissolution of the JTF on November 2.[48] Two days later, the U.S. forces remaining in Grenada transitioned to peacekeeping operations, the third and final phase of Operation Urgent Fury. Battalion-sized elements from the 1st Support Command-Forward (1SC-FWD) and 3rd Brigade, 82nd Airborne Division (3/82ABN) executed civil affairs assessments, provided medical assistance, completed field sanitation tasks,

---

[44] For descriptions of the operations conducted by SOF and the 2-8 Marines in northern Grenada see Raines Jr., *The Rucksack War,* 333-335 and 441-442.

[45] Colonel Peter J. Boylan, quoted in Raines, Jr., *The Rucksack War,* 472.

[46] Raines, Jr., *The Rucksack War,* 473

[47] Raines, Jr., *The Rucksack War,* 324 and 367.

[48] Raines, Jr., *The Rucksack War,* 476.

and policed the villages around their compounds. During this period—which amounted to three-quarters of the duration of Operation Urgent Fury —soldiers operated in a low-threat environment that allowed for the use of wheeled transportation, reduced personal equipment loads, and decreased mission durations.[49]

On November 21, 1983, at the cost of 12 soldiers KIA and 108 WIA, Operation Urgent Fury ended.[50] Rapid, successful, and decisive—Urgent Fury proved to the nation and the world that the U.S. military no longer suffered from its Vietnam-induced inferiority complex. Additionally, it confirmed the value of joint warfighting on the modern battlefield, which ushered in a new era of tactical and operational thinking within the uniformed services.[51] Nearly a decade later, however, the Presidential Commission would cite the tactical missions, austere living conditions, and number of casualties experienced during Operation Urgent Fury as evidence that "ground combat is no more refined, no less barbaric and no less physically demanding than it has been throughout history."[52] However, in focusing on these extremes, the Presidential Commission marginalized evidence of the U.S. Army's increasing dependence on wheeled transport and extensive logistical support, as well as the overall decrease in the rate of soldiers killed, wounded, or taken prisoner.[53] The deliberate decision to minimize the importance of technology and its

---

[49] Raines, Jr., *The Rucksack War,* 472-476, 484-513.

[50] U.S. Army CMH, "Campaigns of the U.S. Army;" Defense Manpower Data Center, "Worldwide U.S. Active Duty Military Deaths: Selected Military Operations (1980-1996)," Defense Casualty Analysis System, https://www.dmdc.osd.mil/dcas/pages/report_operations.xhtml (accessed November 28, 2012). Of note, the U.S. Army reported no POW during Operation Urgent Fury. For further, see Appendix C, Casualty Rate Comparison.

[51] Stewart, *Operation Urgent Fury,* 36.

[52] Presidential Commission, *Report to the President*, 24-25, 62-63, C-124.

[53] Soldier casualty rates during the 33.2 combat years between 1982-2012 were hundreds of times less than soldier casualty rates during the 35.3 combat years experienced between 1775-

associated doctrine and focus only on the limited experiences of a handful of units is representative of the cognitive dissonance that permeates the entire combat exclusion policy debate. Over ninety of the reported activity during Urgent Fury does not correspond to the conditions of combat assumed by the Presidential Commission.[54] This is not to say that such a preponderance of evidence diminishes the importance of the remaining ten percent; however, neither should this ten percent diminish the validity of the ninety. When viewed in its entirety, Operation Urgent Fury provides little evidence that the revocation of the combat exclusion policy would pose more than a low operational risk to the U.S. Army.

Operation Desert Shield and Desert Storm, Saudi Arabia and Kuwait

Eight years after Operation Urgent Fury, and a short eight months after completing contingency operations in Panama, the United States found itself again embroiled in a war to protect its vital interests abroad. The conflict centered on the tiny state of Kuwait, an obscenely rich Arab nation that benefitted immensely from its geographic position as the "door to the entire oil-producing [Persian Gulf] region."[55] What Kuwait touted in riches, however, it sorely lacked in military strength. Consequently, its northern neighbor, the Republic of Iraq, increasingly viewed the invasion and annexation of Kuwait as a swift and lucrative method of managing its own burgeoning fiscal crisis.[56] Thinly veiling these financial motives in a cloak of pan-Arabism, Iraqi

---

1981. For further see Appendix C, Casualty Rate Comparison.

[54] See previous discussion on the downgrading of uniform and threat levels on October 28, 1983, three days after the commencement of hostilities. Operation Urgent Fury lasted a total of 28 days; the period October 25-28 constitutes the 10% of reporting that aligns with the Presidential Commission's assumptions.

[55] Frank N. Schubert and Theresa L. Kraus, eds., *The Whirlwind War: The United States Army in Operations DESERT SHIELD and DESERT STORM* (Washington, D.C.: Center of Military History, 1995), 21.

[56] For a brief summary of the Iraqi motivations for the annexation of Kuwait, see: United

18

President Saddam Hussein signaled his intent to invade Kuwait in both diplomatic and public

information forums as early as February 1990.[57] However, the launch of over 140,000 Iraqi

troops and 3,000 tanks, infantry vehicles, artillery pieces, and logistical trucks across the Iraq-

Kuwait border at 0200 hours on August 2, 1990, still surprised almost every nation in the world.[58]

The U.S. response to the Iraqi aggression was immediate; President George H. W. Bush

publically condemned the invasion during a press conference at 0845 hours on August 2, where

he called for the "immediate and unconditional withdrawal of all…Iraqi forces [in Kuwait]."[59]

Three days later, Bush dispatched his Secretary of Defense, the Honorable Dick Cheney, U.S.

Central Command (USCENTCOM) Commander-In-Chief (CINCCENT) General H. Norman

Schwarzkopf, and U.S. Army Central (USARCENT) Commander Lieutenant General John J.

Yeosock to the Kingdom of Saudi Arabia to persuade King Fahd bin Abdulaziz Al Saud to

request U.S. assistance in defending his country from future Iraqi aggression.[60] Fahd conceded on

---

States Department of Defense, *Conduct of the Persian Gulf War* (Washington, D.C.: Government
Printing Office, 1992), 1-20; Schubert and Kraus, *The Whirlwind War,* 3-23. For a detailed
discussion of the Iraqi road to war, see: Steve A. Yetiv, *Persian Gulf Crisis* (Westport, CT:
Greenwood Press, 1997).

[57] Dennis R. Mitzel, "When Will We Listen?" (research report, Air War College, April
1997), 6-7.

[58] United States Department of Defense, *Conduct of the Persian Gulf War*, 8; Robert H.
Scales, Jr., *Certain Victory: The U.S. Army in the Gulf War* (Washington, D.C.: Center of
Military History, 1994), 45.

[59] C-SPAN, "Iraqi Invasion of Kuwait," C-SPAN Video Library, 6:00, http://www.c-
spanvideo.org/program/13395-1 (accessed March 10, 2013). For the codification of these
comments, see George H. W. Bush, "Address on Iraq's Invasion of Kuwait," *Public Papers of the
Presidents of the United States* (August 8, 1990),
http://millercenter.org/president/speeches/detail/5529 (accessed March 11, 2013); George H. W.
Bush, National Security Directive 45, "U.S. Policy In Response to the Iraqi Invasion of Kuwait,"
August 20, 1990.

[60] U.S. Army Central is alternately referred to as USARCENT and Third U.S. Army in
much of the literature on Operations Desert Shield and Desert Storm. It is the same unit. For
clarity, USARCENT will be used throughout the remainder of this document. Of note, the U.S.

August 6, and on August 7 Bush authorized the deployment of U.S. military forces to Southwest Asia.[61] The 2nd, 1st, then 3rd Brigades of the 82d Airborne Division (2/82ABN, 1/82ABN, and 3/82ABN, respectively) hastily deployed to the Kingdom from August 8-24, prepared to "deter and counter any Iraqi aggression against Saudi Arabia."[62] Simultaneously, designated U.S. Navy vessels and U.S. Air Force platforms also began making their way to the Gulf.[63] These actions clearly signaled Bush's intent to uphold the Carter Doctrine, a decade old policy that explicitly stated "An attempt by any outside force to gain control of the Persian Gulf region [would] be regarded as an assault on the vital interests of the United States of America," and that "such an assault [would] be repelled by any means necessary, including military force."[64] In essence, despite the defensive rationale behind its initial deployment, the U.S. Army readied for war.

Operation Desert Shield officially began with the deployment of ground combat troops from the United States on August 8, 1990.[65] The concept of the operation was to "defend Saudi

---

Department of the Army officially retired the Third U.S. Army designation in 2008. For additional information, see U.S. Army Central Public Affairs, "Third Army now U.S. Army Central," U.S. Army Central, http://www.centcom.mil/news/third-army-now-u-s-army-central (accessed March 25, 2013)

[61] United States Department of Defense, *Conduct of the Persian Gulf War*, 22; Schubert and Kraus, *The Whirlwind War*, 49-52; Scales, *Certain Victory,* 45-46.

[62] Richard B. Cheney, "Army Operations Update—Information Memorandum Number 1," Memorandum for Secretary of the Army and Chief of Staff of the Army (Washington D.C., August 8, 1990).

[63] United States Department of Defense, *Conduct of the Persian Gulf War*, 22.

[64] Jimmy Carter, "State of the Union Address," *Public Papers of the Presidents of the United States* (January, 28, 1980), http://www.presidency.ucsb.edu/ws/index.php?pid=33079 (accessed March 10, 2013).

[65] United States Department of Defense, *Conduct of the Persian Gulf War*, 44. Of note, the CMH lists August 2, 1990 as the date Operation Desert Shield began, despite the fact that combat forces did not arrive in Saudi Arabia until August 8, 1990.

Arabia with whatever forces were on hand while a buildup of additional forces was occurring."[66]

As the Ground Component Command (GCC), USARCENT met this challenge by planning three

separate operations, code named Desert Dragon I, Desert Dragon II, and Desert Dragon III. The

Desert Dragons were sequential, cumulative operations designed to protect critical Saudi Arabian

infrastructure and serve as a credible deterrent to further Iraqi aggression.

As the first combat unit to arrive in the Kuwaiti Theater of Operations (KTO), 2/82ABN

served as the main effort for Desert Dragon I. They landed in Saudi Arabia on August 9,

immediately establishing a defensive perimeter around Dhahran Air Base and the port of ad-

Dammam.[67] Uncertain of what Hussein's reaction would be to the arrival of American combat

power on his southern flank, 2/82ABN set to work fortifying these key logistical nodes to prevent

Iraqi forces from moving within indirect fire range and enable U.S. follow on forces to flow into

the KTO unmolested.[68] Troops conducted much of this work at night to avoid the intense desert

sun, spending their days rehydrating and attempting to rest in the only area large enough to

contain them—an open field behind the U.S. Military Training Mission to Saudi Arabia.[69] From

August 9-12, the soldiers of 2/82ABN executed Desert Dragon I with the equipment and rations

---

[66] Richard W. Stewart, *War in the Persian Gulf: Operations DESERT SHIELD and DESERT STORM, August 1990-March 1991* (Washington, D.C.: Center of Military History, 2010), 16.

[67] Stewart, *War in the Persian Gulf,* 6-9.

[68] Scales, *Certain Victory,* 82; Stewart, *War in the Persian Gulf,* 7.

[69] Schubert and Kraus, *The Whirlwind War,* 56. At some point during DESERT DRAGON I, the officers of the U.S. Military Training Mission to Saudi Arabia arranged for soldiers to be transported to and housed at a vacant Saudi military building several miles from Dhahran. However, as the field continued to be used to contain troops upon their initial arrival into the KTO, and chronological information is not available to determine exactly when this move occurred, this information is only provided as a footnote. See Schubert and Kraus, 57 for further.

they deployed with.[70] While working, they wore desert camouflage uniforms (DCU), Kevlar

helmets, and a load bearing equipment (LBE) harness. They also kept their weapons, chemical

protective over-garments, and chemical protective masks at arms length. For food, they ate pre-

---

[70] Detailed packing lists for 82d Airborne Division units deploying in support of Operations Desert Shield and Desert Storm could not be located. However, the available evidence supports the inference that these soldiers carried the standard combat load identified in Appendix B, Equipment Weights and Load Calculations. In addition to the standard combat load, all soldiers deployed in support of Operations Desert Shield and Desert Storm carried chemical protective over-garments and chemical protective mask in order to counter the chemical weapon threat posed by Iraq; the total weight of the standard combat and chemical protective load during this period was therefore 95 lbs. See Appendix B for further. Specific support for the accuracy of these calculations can be found in Reginald R. Gooden, "Experiences during Operations Desert Shield/Storm: Operations Desert Shield/Storm, Iraq, 08/12/90 thru 04/01/91, 91B1P, Infantry Platoon Combat Line Medic, A Company, 1/505th PIR, 82d ABN DIV," United States Army Sergeant Majors Academy Personal Experience Papers Collection, Combined Arms Research Library, Fort Leavenworth, KS. Specifically, Gooden states, "once he packed his rucksack, it weighed in excess of 90 pounds." It is important to note that this is the weight of Gooden's rucksack *alone*, indicating that his total combat load was 142.49. This number is obviously higher than the 95 lbs. weight noted earlier in this note. This discrepancy can be accounted for by the fact that Gooden was a combat line medic, who by his own account assisted his platoon in carrying enough "medical supplies [, specifically intravenous (IV) fluids,] to sustain [his unit] for 72 hours." Per the TF Devil CAAT data and the current Medical Equipment Set Combat Medic Support and Consumables Handbook, the modern combat medic carries a medic bag weighing 19.5 lbs., which includes six pairs of patient examining gloves. Given the context of Gooden's statement, we can thus infer that Gooden anticipated treating at least six patients a day for at least three days. We can additionally infer that he prepared to administer the maximum allowable dosage of IV fluids to those patients. Current Defense Health Board and Combat Medic Advanced Skills Training documents indicate that this dosage should not exceed 1000ml (1.3 lbs.) of the crystalloid fluid Hextend or 1000ml (2.4 lbs.) of the crystalloid fluid Ringers Lactate. Based on this information, Gooden likely carried at least 33.3 lbs. of IV fluids. Combined, the medic bag and additional IV fluids totaled 52.8 lbs. Deducting this total from the total weight reported by Gooden returns the non-medical combat load to 89.69 lbs., roughly conforming to the weight of the likely combat load carried by 82d Airborne Division soldiers. Medical references cited include the following: U.S. Army Medical Materiel Agency, *Medical Equipment Set Combat Medic Support and Consumables Handbook: 6545-01-609-2699, UA 246C, LIN U65480* (Fort Detrick, MD: U.S. Army Medical Materiel Agency, January 2013); *Hypovolemic Shock Management: Combat Medic Advanced Skills Training* (brief, 10th Mountain Division, n.d.), slide 44-48; Wayne M. Lednar and Gregory A. Poland, "Recommendations Regarding the Tactical Combat Casualty Care Guidelines on Fluid Resuscitation 2010-07," Memorandum for George Peach Taylor, Jr. M.D., December 10, 2010; Task Force Devil CAAT, *The Modern Warrior's Combat Load,* 109.

packaged meals, called Meal, Ready to Eat (MRE), and supplemented their dietary shortfalls with hamburgers from a Hardee's restaurant near the airport.[71]

What 2/82ABN initially lacked in creature comforts, they more than made up for in firepower. Prior to their departure, XVIII Airborne Corps augmented the forces assigned to deploy with the 2/82ABN in order to mitigate the limitations inherent in the structure of any regular light infantry brigade.[72] Consequently, within days of arriving, 2/82ABN received not only several of their organic tube-launched, optical-tracked, wire-guided (TOW) missile-equipped High Mobility Multipurpose Wheeled Vehicles (HMMWV), but also an additional M551 (Sheridan) tank company, battalion of Apache attack helicopters, battalion of 105mm howitzers, and Multiple-Launch Rocket System (MLRS) platoon.[73] The arrival of these assets heralded the end of Desert Dragon I, as they provided 2/82ABN the capacity necessary to execute Desert Dragon II.

On August 12, 2/82ABN expanded the American "toehold" in Saudi Arabia into a "foothold" during Desert Dragon II.[74] During the operation, 4th Battalion, 325th Airborne Infantry Regiment (4-325IN) "moved north 110 miles to occupy the port of al-Jubayl in order to protect the arrival of the 7th Marine Expeditionary Brigade," while a second infantry battalion established Forward Operating Base (FOB) Essex near the Saudi Arabian city of An Nu'ayriyah, roughly 200 miles to the northwest.[75] The establishment of FOB Essex was a key defensive move within the

---

[71] Schubert and Kraus, *The Whirlwind War,* 53, 65.

[72] For an analysis of the strengths and weaknesses of the light infantry brigade, see Ray B. Johnson, Scott Campbell, Mark E. Moore, Frankie Marrero, and Sue Parnell-Smith, "The Light Infantry Division" (group paper, United States Army Sergeant Majors Academy, 2005), 6.

[73] Scales, *Certain Victory,* 82.

[74] Scales, *Certain Victory,* 84.

[75] Scales, *Certain Victory,* 86. For reference, 1st Battalion, 325th Infantry Regiment (1-325

23

KTO. Its size and location supported the forward deployment of U.S. Army close combat attack (CCA) aviation assets, which provided a first strike capability against any encroaching Iraqi forces and thus dramatically increased freedom of maneuver for the rapidly growing number of U.S. and coalition forces arriving at Dhahran, ad-Dammam, and al-Jubayl. Logistical relief also accompanied the influx of combat forces. On August 17, four ships containing "pre-positioned stocks of equipment" arrived in ad-Dammam, providing enough supplies to "[stabilize] most of the immediate crises" facing the troops operating within the KTO.[76] By August 19, host nation logistical support also began to flow. During this period, Saudi Arabia provided an astounding 1.5 million gallons of water, 270,000 meals, 13,530 vehicles, 2,700 latrines, 2,250 shower units, and

---

IN), 2nd Battalion, 325th Infantry Regiment (2-325 IN), and 4-325 IN were the three infantry battalions subordinate to 2/82 ABN for the duration of Operations Desert Shield and Desert Storm.

[76] Schubert and Kraus, *The Whirlwind War,* 59. Specifically, Schubert and Kraus report that these ships, which "had been anchored off the coast of Diego Garcia[,] brought rations, cots, tents, blankets, and medical supplies, as well as refrigerated trailers, reverse-osmosis water-purification units, forklifts, and tactical petroleum terminals." Additionally, it is important to note that the personal equipment and rations arriving in theater with units who had deployed after the 82d Airborne Division were quantitatively different. These items were what U.S. Department of the Army FM 21-18 terms sustainment loads. For further information, see U.S. Department of the Army, FM 21-18, *Foot Marches* (Washington, D.C.: U.S. Department of the Army, 1990), 5-1 – 5-17. For information on the average composition and weight of these sustainment loads, see Appendix B, Equipment Weights and Load Calculations. Specifically with regard to Operation Desert Storm, the most detailed sustainment load packing list can be found in Stephen A. Bourque and John W. Burdan III, *The Road to Safwan: The 1st Squadron, 4th Cavalry in the 1991 Persian Gulf War* (Denton, TX: University of North Texas Press, 2007), 31. Specifically, Bourque and Burdan reference the personal notes of Debra L. Anderson, who served as a member of the 1st Infantry Division G1 during the pre-deployment and deployment operations of 1st Squadron, 4th Cavalry Regiment (1-4 CAV). Bourque and Burdan's summary of Anderson's notes state that "each soldier had four uniforms with all patches and name tags sewn on, two pairs of boots, eight pairs of socks, six pairs of under shorts, two field jackets, his web gear to carry his pack, two canteens, a sleeping bag, shelter half, chemical protective over-garments, protective mask, helmet, and so on and so forth." Using the data provided by the TF Devil CAAT, those items listed in addition to the standard soldier combat load totaled 25.81 lbs., increasing the 1ID soldier's combat load to 120.81 lbs. Unlike 2/82 ABN units, however, 1ID soldiers spread their gear between "two duffel bags and a rucksack," which they moved by truck to their housing area, where it remained for the majority of their time in Saudi Arabia.

40,000 bundles of laundry to U.S. troops per day. Additionally, the Saudi government made available the use of large festival tents, high-rise apartment buildings, and commercial warehouses to provide soldiers respite from the brutal desert sun and sand.[77] Desert Dragon II continued until September 1, when XVIII Airborne Corps "ordered the 101st Airborne Division (Air Assault) (101 AASLT) to relieve 2/82ABN at FOB Essex."[78] In all, Desert Dragon II enabled the reception, staging, and onward integration (RSOI) of such a significant amount of combat power that the USARCENT commander declared himself "confident in [the unit's] ability to detect and punish a major armored attack."[79]

Desert Dragon III began two days later, on September 3, when the 101 AASLT established Area of Operations (AO) Normandy, north of the re-christened FOB Bastogne (formerly FOB Essex).[80] From FOB Bastogne, the attack aviation and long-range artillery of the 101 AASLT prepared to attack the forward echelons of any Iraqi forces bold enough to cross the Kuwaiti-Saudi Arabian border. Behind them, the recently arrived and heavily armored 24th Infantry Division (24ID) positioned themselves to destroy any forces that escaped the 101 AASLT's onslaught. The brigades of the 82d ABN DIV returned to their defensive positions around the critical infrastructure of at Dhahran, ad-Dammam, and al-Jubayl to protect the flow of logistical and combat units still arriving in theater.[81] Desert Dragon III culminated in early October, having successfully established the "shield" for which the larger operation is named.

---

[77] Schubert and Krause, *The Whirlwind War,* 62.

[78] Scales, *Certain Victory,* 92.

[79] Scales, *Certain Victory,* 86. For reference, by August 30, the U.S. Army had deployed over 40,000 soldiers, 237 helicopters and 5700 vehicles to the KTO. See also Schubert and Kraus, 59 for further information on the arrival of troops and equipment during the month of August.

[80] Scales, *Certain Victory,* 91-92.

[81] Scales, *Certain Victory,* 92-93.

Over the next three months, an additional 250,000 American troops arrived, trained, and

deployed to forward defensive positions under the protection established by the Desert Dragon

operations.[82] As time passed, living conditions dramatically improved throughout the KTO, most

significantly for those units furthest from the Iraqi-Saudi Arabian border.[83] For example, bases

such as Camp Eagle II [located near King Fahd International Airport (KFIA)] gained thousands

of tents, latrines, showers, as well as movie theaters, telephone banks, and a Post Exchange (PX).

Conversely, soldiers rotating through the sandy desolation of FOB Bastogne found themselves

living out of foxholes and using "MRE boxes as pillows."[84] Regardless of their sleeping

arrangements, soldiers throughout the KTO had one thing in common—they spent the majority of

their waking hours preparing to defend Saudi Arabia from the imminent threat posed by forty-

three Iraqi armored and infantry divisions arrayed along southwestern borders of Iraq and

Kuwait.[85] Ultimately, no attack came from these forces; unfortunately, this did not prevent the

loss of American life. According to the Defense Casualty Analysis System, as Operation Desert

---

[82] Bourque and Burdan, *The Road to Safwan*, 113; Schubert and Kraus, *The Whirlwind War*, 62.

[83] For detailed discussion of soldier activities and living conditions during this period, see: Edward M. Flanagan, Jr., *Lightning: The 101st in the Gulf War* (Washington: Brassey's, Inc., 1994), 59-100; William J. Bolt, "Command Report, 101st Airborne Division (Air Assault) for operations Desert Shield and Desert Storm, 2 August 1990 through 1 May 1991," Memorandum for Commander, XVIII Airborne Corps (Fort Campbell, KY, July 1, 1991) and U.S. General Accounting Office, *Report to the Secretary of Defense: Women in the Military, Deployment in the Persian Gulf War*, by Foy D. Wicker, Marilyn Mauch, Beverly Ann Bendekgey, Kathleen M. Joyce, Julio Luna, and David Moser, Report to the Secretary of Defense, Washington D.C., July 1993.

[84] Flanagan, Jr., *Lightning,* 84, 60-61, 66; Bolt, "Command Report," 18-19.

[85] Schubert and Kraus, *The Whirlwind War,* 135.

Shield drew to a close on January 15, 1991, the U.S. Army had already suffered 21 soldier deaths from non-hostile causes.[86]

Operation Desert Storm, the military mission to liberate Kuwait, began with the scream of HELLFIRE missiles fired by a company of U.S. Army Apache helicopters at 0238 hours on January 17, 1991.[87] Immediately following the Apache onslaught, U.S. Air Force attack aircraft penetrated Iraqi airspace and proceeded to pummel exposed Iraqi military units and infrastructure.[88] For the next five weeks, the U.S. Air Force executed thousands of aerial attack and bombing missions throughout Iraq in an attempt to reduce overall Iraqi combat effectiveness and mask the repositioning of U.S. Army ground combat and logistical forces. The U.S. Army prepared for the upcoming ground invasion by conducting limited reconnaissance and indirect fire operations along the Iraqi-Saudi Arabian border.[89] Specifically, armored reconnaissance patrols from the 3rd Armored Cavalry Regiment (3ACR) probed Iraqi defenses along border, while artillery batteries from the 1st Infantry Division (1ID) and 1st Cavalry Division (1CD) relentlessly bombarded Iraqi formations with thousands of pounds of ordnance. Additionally, just behind USARCENT's forward line of own troops (FLOT) the 22d Support Command (22SUPCOM) "logged about 1.2 million miles per week" moving men and materiel north to

---

[86] Defense Manpower Data Center, "U.S. Military Casualties – Persian Gulf War Casualty Summary Desert Shield," Defense Casualty Analysis System, https://www.dmdc.osd.mil/dcas/pages/report_gulf_shield.xhtml (accessed March 12, 2013).

[87] Bolt, "Command Report," 13-14; Flanagan, Jr., *Lightning,* 115-133. See also Colin L. Powell, U.S. CJCS, "Execute Order for Operation DESERT STORM," Washington D.C., January 15, 1991.

[88] Schubert and Kraus, *The Whirlwind War,* 155-171.

[89] Richard M. Swain, *"Lucky War:" Third Army in Desert Storm* (Fort Leavenworth, KS: U.S. Army Command and General Staff College Press, 1990), 197-206; Schubert and Kraus, *The Whirlwind War,* 170.

establish logistical supply bases capable of supporting continued offensive operations.[90] In all, these efforts resulted in the reduction of Iraqi frontline and reserve units to less than 50% strength and the maneuvering of more than two corps of U.S. military might into favorable assault positions by February 23, 1990.[91]

The "ground assault to liberate Kuwait," began at 0400 hours on February 24, 1990 and famously lasted for just 100 hours.[92] In accordance with the CINCCENT Operation Plan (OPLAN) for Operation Desert Storm, units attacked into Iraq as if aligned along the invisible spoke of a "Great Wheel."[93] Arrayed along the southwestern border of Iraq, USARCENT forces were the furthest from the hub of the wheel. The first of its major subordinate commands, XVIII Airborne Corps, conducted "a supporting attack to block east-west LOCs...[within southern Iraq] to isolate Iraqi forces in the [KTO];" the second, VII Corps, attacked "north...along the western Kuwait border to destroy Republican Guard forces."[94] On USARCENT's eastern flank, Joint Forces Command-North (JFC-N), U.S. Marine Central Command (MARCENT), JFC-East (JFC-E)—each progressively closer to the hub of the wheel—attacked north to destroy Iraqi forces in

---

[90] Schubert and Kraus, *The Whirlwind War,* 160-163.

[91] For information on the attrition of Iraqi forces during the Operation Desert Storm air war, see United States Department of Defense, *Conduct of the Persian Gulf War,* 353; Schubert and Kraus, *The Whirlwind War,* 166. For information on the repositioning of U.S. combat power prior to the commencement of ground offensive operations, see United States Department of Defense, *Conduct of the Persian Gulf War,* 336, 341; Flanagan, Jr., *Lightning,* 135-147.

[92] United States Department of Defense, *Conduct of the Persian Gulf War,* 358; Scales, *Certain Victory,* 216, 316.

[93] Scales, *Certain Victory,* 145-150.

[94] Headquarters, USCENTCOM, Riyadh, Saudi Arabia, APO NY 09852, 16 December 1990, USCINCCENT OPLAN for Operation Desert Storm, 14 and 18, quoted in Swain, *Lucky War,* 207. Emphasis in original.

Kuwait.[95] For four days and four nights, American and coalition units throughout the KTO attacked towards their objectives in accordance with the larger USCENTCOM OPLAN.[96] Notably, however, each did so using unique methods of attack and facing distinctly different amounts of enemy resistance. Specific examination of USARCENT's air assault, obstacle breaching, and ground maneuver operations provide excellent examples of the variety of missions and equipment used by soldiers during the ground combat portion of Operation Desert Storm.

As the first major maneuver of ground invasion, the XVIII Airborne Corps ordered the 101 AASLT to seize a large clearing 100km into Iraq and establish a forward operating base (FOB) code named Cobra.[97] XVIII Airborne Corps specifically chose the 101 AASLT for this mission, as the unit's unique air assault capability would allow it to quickly mass combat power deep in enemy territory, shocking Iraqi troops in the area and deceiving the Iraqi Republican Guard Corps (IRGC) as to the location of the USCENTCOM main attack. 1st Brigade, 101st AASLT (1/101 AASLT) successfully executed the task, deploying roughly "200 aircraft…2050 soldiers, 50 TOWs, two artillery batteries, and [their] Command and Control people and equipment," in less than three hours.[98] Once on the ground, 1/101 AASLT's infantry battalions cleared the 200km area allotted for FOB Cobra using a mixture of foot, vehicle, and helicopter patrols to find and destroy Iraqi troops. Simultaneously, artillery batteries emplaced their guns

---

[95] United States Department of Defense, *Conduct of the Persian Gulf War*, 338. As these units were primarily comprised of coalition and non-U.S. Army forces, they are not included in further analysis of this conflict.

[96] Swain, *Lucky War*, 225-318; Flanagan, Jr., *Lightning*, 165-221; Scales, *Certain Victory*, 213-320; Bourque and Burdan, *The Road to Safwan*, 113-184; Stephen A. Bourque, *Jayhawk! The VII Corps in the Persian Gulf War* (Washington D.C.: U.S. Department of the Army, 2002), 223-384.

[97] Scales, *Certain Victory*, 217.

[98] Flanagan, Jr., *Lightning*, 171; Bolt, "Command Report," 25.

and sustainment soldiers established fuel and ammunition resupply points within the developing

perimeter. During these operations, soldiers wore a helmet, body armor, and chemical protective

suit; each also carried a chemical protective mask, a basic load of ammunition, MREs, and water,

as well as their personal weapon. Within fourteen hours, FOB Cobra was secure and

operational.[99]

The following day, 3rd Brigade, 101 AASLT (3/101 AASLT) repeated the success of 1-

101 AASLT further north, establishing key blocking positions along a 300 km stretch of Iraqi

Highway 8.[100] 3/101 AASLT used many of the same tactics as 1/101 AASLT; however, since the

depth of this second penetration was well beyond the current reach of the USARCENT logistical

system, 3/101 AASLT soldiers carried the added burden of two to three times their basic load of

ammunition and rations.[101] 3/101 AASLT also operated for over 24-hours with only a portion of

its assigned firepower and maneuver platforms after inclement weather delayed the deployment

of over half the brigade from its Tactical Assembly Area (TAA) in Saudi Arabia.[102] Despite these

minor setbacks, however, the 101 AASLT operations were an unqualified success. Unfortunately,

they did not come without cost.

---

[99] Flanagan, Jr., *Lightning*, 173, 176; Bolt, "Command Report," 24-25.

[100] Flanagan, Jr., *Lightning*, 181.

[101] Flanagan, Jr., *Lightning*, 179-190; Thomas Houlahan, *Gulf War: The Complete History* (New London, NH: Schrenker Military Publishing, 1999), 249; 3rd Brigade, 101st Airborne Division (Air Assault), *Operation DESERT SHIELD / Operation DESERT STORM Yearbook* (Paducha, KY: Turner Publishing Company, 1992), 22-23 and 59. It is imperative to note that while soldiers did indeed need to carry these immense rucksacks forward in order to sustain themselves on the battlefield, they were routinely placed in vehicles or left in the care of sustainment personnel during the conduct of offensive operations. In other words, the only period in which soldiers labored under the total weight of their gear was boarding, riding in, de-boarding their aircraft. Houlahan, *Gulf War*, 246-247 and Swain, *Lucky War*, 242-243.

[102] Flanagan, Jr., *Lightning*, 188; Bolt, "Command Report," 28; Houlahan, *Gulf War*, 249-250; Swain, *Lucky War*, 241-243.

The highest profile losses within the 101 AASLT occurred on February 27, when Iraqi antiaircraft fire disabled a Combat Search and Rescue (CSAR) helicopter enroute to recover an F-16 pilot who had ejected over the southern Iraqi city of Basra. Having suffered extensive damage, the CSAR helicopter crashed, instantly killing five of the eight crewmembers aboard. The three remaining crewmembers sustained significant injuries and were immediately taken prisoner by Iraqi forces. Given the concerns of the Presidential Commission regarding likely discrepancies between the treatment of male and female captives, it is necessary to highlight that the single female POW taken from the CSAR crash site, Major Rhonda Cornum, was molested by an Iraqi soldier in the presence of a male POW on the first day of her capture. Per Cornum's account, the only reason the Iraqi did not rape her was she because she screamed when he re-injured the arm she had broken in the crash. Little information is available on the treatment of the two male POWs; it is unknown whether they suffered similar sexual trauma. Iraqi forces repatriated all three POWs taken from the CSAR helicopter crash site immediately following the military cease-fire on March 3.[103]

While the 101 AASLT made their "rendezvous with destiny" 300km to the north, the 1st Infantry Division (1ID) took much more difficult path toward the enemy.[104] At 0530 hours on February 24, the division crept north in mixture M1 Abrams tanks, M3A2 Bradley Fighting

---

[103] Presidential Commission, *Report to the President*, 25; Bolt, 'Command Report," 30-31; Flanagan, Jr., *Lightning*, 211-221; Rhonda Cornum, unknown interviewer, *Frontline*, PBS, n.d., http://www.pbs.org/wgbh/pages/frontline/gulf/war/5.html (accessed March 25, 2013); Suzanne Seixas, "A Soldier Without Fortune: Ex-P.O.W. Troy Dunlap returns to a hero's welcome, a new baby—and $18,000 of debt," CNN Money, May 1, 1991, http://money.cnn.com/magazines/moneymag/moneymag_archive/1991/05/01/86516/index.htm (accessed March 25, 2013); Russell Sellers, "Post Honors Outstanding Employee," U.S. Army, http://www.army.mil/article/67629/Post_honors_outstanding_employee/ (accessed March 23, 2013).

[104] MG William C. Lee, quoted by 101st Airborne Division (Air Assault), "101st Airborne Division History," 101st Airborne Division Homepage, http://www.campbell.army.mil/units/101st/Pages/History.aspx (accessed March 14, 2013).

Vehicles (BFV), M577 Command Post Carriers, and TOW-equipped HMMWVs and began to breach the obstacle belt emplaced by the Iraqi 26th Infantry Division along the Saudi Arabia-Iraq border.[105] By 1000 hours, the division had cleared multiple 25km-long lanes into Iraqi territory; unfortunately, they had done it more than nine hours ahead of the schedule established in the VII Corps OPORD.[106] In order to allow the other units along the spoke of the Great Wheel to catch up, VII Corps ordered the division to pause just 4km short of the major Iraqi defensive line.[107] Some soldiers took advantage of the operational pause to adjust their uniforms, attempting to cool down by removing their DCUs or flight suits from beneath their chemical protective suit. As always, soldiers carried their Kevlars, LBEs, and chemical masks at all times.[108] Finally, at 1500 this "solid wall of fire and iron" lurched forward once again.[109] Determined resistance by the Iraqis meant little; the main guns and plows of 1ID's BFVs and tanks sliced through the enemy formations, killing anything that moved and burying the rest alive. Within thirty minutes, 1ID had opened 12 dual capacity and four logistical lanes into Iraq; by 1200 hours the following day, they held battle positions north of the Iraqi trench line.[110] It is important to note that during each stage of this operation, 1ID soldiers fought from their vehicles—either leveraging the superior

---

[105] Bourque and Burdan, *The Road to Safwan*, 25, 47, 53, 106.

[106] Bourque and Burdan, *The Road to Safwan*, 115, 119.

[107] Bourque and Burdan, *The Road to Safwan*, 121.

[108] David Norton, "Cecil's Ride: A Tank Platoon Leader In Desert Storm," *Armor* 113, no. 6 (November-December 1999): 35; Bourque and Burdan, *The Road to Safwan*, 117, photograph 7, photograph 10, photograph 12, photograph 14. For further information regarding the weight of these items, see Appendix B.

[109] Bourque and Burdan, *The Road to Safwan*, 119-123.

[110] Countermine Counter Booby Trap Center, "Operation DESERT SHIELD and Operation DESERT STORM Lessons Learned" (After Action Review, n.d.), 16; Houlahan, *Gulf War*, 289; Bourque and Burdan, *The Road to Safwan*, 127-133; Scales, *Certain Victory*, 229-232.

firepower of the M1 and BFV or firing their personal weapons from the relative protection of an armored platform.[111]

Similarly, units maneuvering to attack the main combat forces of the Iraqi Army also employed their armored vehicles to the greatest extent possible. From February 24-28, the 3d Armored Cavalry Regiment (3ACR), 24th Infantry Division (24ID), 2d Armored Cavalry Regiment (2ACR), 1st Armored Division (1AD), 3rd Armored Division (3AD), and 1st Cavalry Division (1CD) all engaged in major battles across the KTO. The number and complexity of these operations render a detailed examination of each impossible in this format; however, certain experiences were common to all engagements. Most significantly, every unit maneuvered and fought using mounted formations.[112] For one hundred hours, task-organized battalions of M1 tanks, BFVs, M113 Armored Personnel Carriers (APC), and TOW-equipped HMMWVs swept across the Iraqi desert, shifting between traveling over watch and attack formations as if conducting a deadly ballet.[113] Crews of three to four soldiers propelled these units forward.

---

[111] Bourque and Burdan, *The Road to Safwan,* 123-124.

[112] For a timeline and broad overview of ground force maneuvers during Operation Desert Storm, see: Swain, *Lucky War,* 243-265; Scales, *Certain Victory,* 237-313; Houlahan, *Gulf War,* 251-272, 319-332, 355-409. (For reference, the major battles identified in these works include al-Busayyah, 73 Easting, Norfolk, and Medina Ridge.) For detailed information on the operations of 2ACR and 3ACR, see: Vince Crawley, "Ghost Troop's Battle at the 73 Easting," *Armor* 100, no. 3 (May-June 1991): 7-12; John Hillen, "2d Armored Cavalry: The Campaign to Liberate Kuwait," *Armor* 100, no. 4 (July-August 1991): 8-12; A.A. Puryear and Gerald R. Haywood, II, "Ar Rumaylah Airfield Succumbs to Hasty Attack," *Armor* 100, no. 5 (September-October 1991): 16-20; Lon E. Maggart, "A Leap of Faith," *Armor* 101, no. 1 (January-February 1992): 24-32; Richard M. Bohannon, "Dragon's Roar: 1-37 Armor in the Battle of 73 Easting," *Armor* 101, no. 3 (May-June 1992): 11-17; Daniel L. Davis, "The 2d ACR at the Battle of 73 Easting," *Field Artillery* (April 1992): 48-53.

[113] During Operation Desert Storm, the foremost USARCENT units successfully maneuvered over 190 miles north and 70 miles east. These maneuvers also occurred rapidly; 1 AD, for example, "advanced 144 kilometers in sixteen hours of maneuver and combat, a cumulative rate of 9 kilometers an hour." See Schubert and Kraus, *The Whirlwind War,* 201 and Swain, *Lucky War,* 245 for further. For a detailed discussion of U.S. Army forms of maneuver and movement techniques, see U.S. Department of the Army, *Offense and Defense,* ADRP 3-90,

Crouched in the cramped cabins of their vehicles, these teams sprang into action at any sign of enemy forces—loading and reloading rounds weighing upwards of 54-pounds into the breeches of their main guns in as little as two-seconds.[114] Once engaged in direct combat, the duration of the battle varied in accordance with the skill and determination of the opposing forces. At 73 Easting, for example, soldiers assigned to Eagle Troop, 2nd Squadron, 2 ACR (E/2-2ACR) fought for only 23 minutes. Further east, the Iraqi Medina Brigade kept 1st Brigade, 1 AD (1/1 AD) engaged for over six hours.[115] Regardless, the outcome of every engagement across the KTO was the same—the surrender or destruction of the Iraqi force in contact.

Offensive ground combat operations in the KTO officially ended at 0800 hours on February 28; three days later the Republic of Iraq agreed to a military cease-fire.[116] Immediately, the mission of U.S. Army units in the KTO shifted to peace enforcement and humanitarian aid. Troops worked tirelessly to destroy abandoned Iraqi ordnance and military equipment and provide aid to Iraqi refugees, as well as salvage and rebuild what remained of Kuwait's infrastructure. They executed these missions on a rotational basis, returning frequently to the safety and comfort of their Saudi Arabian FOBs and base camps.[117]

(Washington, D.C.: Department of the Army, August 31, 2012), 3-7, 5-5. For a graphical depiction of the typical division formation used during Operation Desert Storm, see Scales, *Certain Victory,* 239.

[114] For two vignettes of experiences reported by tank crews during Operation Desert Storm, see Scales, *Certain Victory,* 1-4, 213-215.

[115] Scales, *Certain Victory,* 4, 296-300; Swain, *Lucky War,* 263-264; Houlahan, *Gulf War,* 401-408.

[116] Swain, *Lucky War,* 319; Scales, *Certain Victory,* 322-323.

[117] Scales, *Certain Victory,* 323-337. For a complete treatment of U.S. Army activities from March 3 to April 7, 1991, see Janet A. McDonnell, *After DESERT STORM: The U.S. Army and the Reconstruction of Kuwait* (Washington, D.C.: Department of the Army, 1999).

Operation Desert Storm officially ended on April 7, 1991, with the formal acceptance of the UN-cease fire conditions by the Republic of Iraq.[118] Years of training, months of preparation, and hours of fighting had delivered the U.S. Army its first decisive major combat victory since World War II. It was a watershed moment, and it unquestionably heralded the benefits of incorporating technology into existing military doctrine and tactics.[119] Such success remained bittersweet, however. A total of 98 U.S. Army soldiers lost their lives in direct combat during the 100-hour battle to liberate Kuwait, 354 were WIA, and five returned to duty after being taken prisoner by Iraqi forces.[120] These losses served as a stark reminder of the risks continually faced by U.S. soldiers. However, the fact that these numbers were significantly lower than the tens of thousands of casualties anticipated at the outset of the campaign indicate that the U.S. Army was willing and able to effectively employ offensive technology and defensive protective measures to achieve mission success. As a result, Operation Desert Storm supports the contention that revoking the combat exclusion policy poses a low operational risk to U.S. Army operations.

Operation Allied Force and Joint Guardian, Kosovo

Having easily defeated the Iraqi Army in 1990-91, the U.S. Army quickly re-deployed its soldiers to the United States. However, before these troops had cleared the last of the desert sand from their rifles, the rise of another violent dictator threatened to draw America back into war. In June 1991, Serbian President Slobodan Milosevic's longstanding attempts to exert control over

---

[118] Scales, *Certain Victory*, 393.

[119] Schubert and Kraus, *The Whirlwind War*, 233-234.

[120] Defense Manpower Data Center, "Principal Wars in Which the United States Participated – U.S. Military Personnel Serving and Casualties (1775-1991)," Defense Casualty Analysis System, https://www.dmdc.osd.mil/dcas/pages/report_principal_wars.xhtml (accessed March 18, 2012); United States Department of Defense, *Conduct of the Persian Gulf War*, A-3 – A-13.

several former Yugoslavian provinces plunged the Balkan Peninsula into conflict. With

increasing ferocity, Milosevic lead Serbia into wars of self-determination with Slovenia, Croatia,

Macedonia, and Bosnia and Herzegovina.[121] Each of these efforts ultimately proved unsuccessful;

however, they introduced a level of ethnic hatred never before seen in the region.[122] In 1998 and

1999, Milosevic capitalized on this sentiment, unleashing the Serbian military on the ethnic

Albanian population of Kosovo in an effort to reassert Serbian Muslim dominance in the Balkans.

For fifteen months, Serbian forces conducted a systematic campaign of ethnic cleansing

throughout Kosovo. On Milosevic's orders, they murdered thousands of Albanian Kosovars and

destroyed millions of dollars in property. On March 23, 1999, after repeated attempts to find a

diplomatic solution to the conflict, the North Atlantic Council of the North Atlantic Treaty

Organization (NATO) agreed that military force was necessary to stop the violence.[123]

---

[121] *Encyclopedia Britannica Online*, s.v. "Slobodan Milosevic,"
http://www.britannica.com/EBchecked/topic/383076/Slobodan-Milosevic (accessed March 16,
2013). For a detailed history of the recent conflicts within the Balkan states prior to Operation
Allied Force, see Christopher Bennett, *Yugoslavia's Bloody Collapse: Causes, Course, and
Consequences* (Washington Square, NY: New York University Press, 1995); Steven L. Berg and
Paul S. Shoup, *The War in Bosnia-Herzegovina: Ethnic Conflict and International Intervention*
(Armonk, NY: M.E. Sharp, 1999); R. Craig Nation, *War in the Balkans: 1991-2002* (Washington
D.C.: Strategic Studies Institute, 2003); Laura Silber and Allan Little, *Yugoslavia: Death of a
Nation* (U.S.: TV Books, 1995).

[122] Author Noel Malcolm goes to great lengths to disprove the common narrative of
"ancient ethnic hatreds" among the peoples of the Balkans. See Noel Malcolm, *Kosovo: A Short
History* (New York, NY: HarperPerennial, 1999) for further. For a general overview of the end
states of these conflicts, see *Encyclopedia Britannica Online*, s.v. "Dayton Accords,"
http://www.britannica.com/EBchecked/topic/153203/Dayton-Accords (accessed March 17,
2013); Richard W. Stewart, ed., *American Military History Volume II*, 439-445.

[123] U.S. Department of Defense, *Report to Congress: Kosovo/Operation ALLIED FORCE
After Action Report, 31 January, 2000"* (Washington, D.C.: Government Printing Office, 2000),
1-3; Bruce R. Nardulli, Walter L. Perry, Bruce Pirnie, John Gordon IV, and John G. McGinn,
Disjointed War: Military Operations in Kosovo, 1999 (Santa Monica, CA: RAND, 2002), 13-19;
Ivo H. Daalder and Michael E. O'Hanlon, *Winning Ugly: NATO's War to Save Kosovo*
(Washington, D.C.: Brookings Institution Press, 2000), 22-100; Wesley K. Clark, *Waging
Modern War* (New York, NY: PublicAffairs, 2001), 131-189; R. Cody Phillips, *Operation JOINT
GUARDIAN: The U.S. Army in Kosovo* (Washington, D.C.: Center of Military History, 2007), 9-

Operation Allied Force, the NATO mission to "arrest the ability of the Serbs to brutally attack the Kosovar Albanians," began on March 24, 1999. The United States committed 725 U.S. Air Force strike and bomber aircraft to the NATO operation, tasking them to destroy Serbian military facilities, logistical centers, and civil infrastructure.[124] Ten days later, U.S. President Bill Clinton agreed to deploy of a small contingent of U.S. Army helicopters and long-range artillery assets to nearby Albania; however, Clinton expressly forbade the use of these units in direct ground combat.[125] Christened Task Force (TF) Hawk by its commander, LTG John W. Hendrix, this element consisted of 24 attack helicopters, 30 utility helicopters, 27 MRLS, and 14 howitzer artillery pieces. To protect these assets, Hendrix received one mechanized infantry battalion task force (equipped with BFVs and M1 tanks), one dismounted infantry battalion task force (equipped with HMMWVs), and separate military police, engineer, and signal companies.[126]

---

10. For a complete chronology of the events leading up to Operation Allied Force, see U.S. Library of Congress, Congressional Research Service, *Kosovo Conflict Chronology: September 1998 – March 1999* by Julie Kim (Washington, D.C.: The Service, 1999).

[124] U.S. Library of Congress, Congressional Research Service, *Kosovo: U.S. and Allied Military Operations* by Steve Bowman (Washington, D.C.: The Service, 2000), Summary; Nardulli, et al., *Disjointed War*, 24, 31-35, 44-56.

[125] Charles E. Kirkpatrick, *"Ruck It Up! The Post-Cold War Transformation of V Corps, 1990-2001* (Washington, D.C.: Department of the Army, 2006), 467-476; Nardulli, et al., *Disjointed War*, 59, 61. For evidence of Clinton's intent to execute Operation Allied Force without the use of ground troops, see William J. Clinton, "Statement on Kosovo," *Public Papers of the Presidents of the United States* (March 24, 1999), http://millercenter.org/president/speeches/detail/3932 (accessed March 17, 2013); William J. Clinton, interview by Dan Rather, *CBS News*, CBS, March 31, 1999; Kenneth Bacon, "U.S. Department of Defense News Briefing, March 23, 1999," U.S. Department of Defense Office of the Assistant Secretary of Defense (Public Affairs), http://www.defense.gov/transcripts/transcript.aspx?transcriptid=632 (accessed March 17, 2013).

[126] Peter W. Rose II and Keith Flowers, "Task Force HAWK Command and Control," *Joint Center for Lessons Learned Bulletin* 2, no. 2 (June 2000): 2-3; Nardulli, et al., *Disjointed War*, 73-75; U.S. Department of Defense, *Report to Congress: Kosovo/Operation ALLIED FORCE After Action Report,* 42-43.

The first soldiers of TF Hawk arrived at the Tirana-Rinas Airport in Albania on April 5, 1999, followed closely by the entirety of 1st Battalion, 6th Infantry Regiment (1-6IN) on April 8. Prepared to land under fire, these soldiers were shocked to find themselves calmly disembarking their C-17 transport aircraft threatened only by the rain.[127] Immediately, commanders set their troops to work unloading the pallets of supplies and equipment that had accompanied them on their trip. A lack of existing infrastructure at the airfield forced soldiers to perform much of the work by hand; what transport vehicles they did procure quickly turned the soft soil of the airfield into a "sea of mud."[128] Initial living conditions at Tirana-Rinas were no better than the working conditions. Having deliberately chosen not to bring their tents, 1-6 IN soldiers had little choice but to sleep in the rain and mud on the outskirts of the airfield.[129] Miserable, but determined, these early arrivals labored day and night to receive the remainder of TF Hawk's personnel and equipment. They supervised contractors delivering and emplacing road construction material from neighboring Macedonia, waded through waist deep mud bogs to shepherd vehicles from aircraft to motor pools, and provided for the physical security of the developing base camp.[130] By April 26, conditions at Tirana-Rinas had improved dramatically, and Hendrix had enough personnel and functioning equipment on hand to declare his 5100-soldier task force fully mission capable (FMC).[131]

---

[127] Kirkpatrick, *Ruck it Up,* 477-479.

[128] U.S. Department of Defense, *Report to Congress: Kosovo/Operation ALLIED FORCE After Action Report,* 37, 40; Kirkpatrick, *Ruck it Up,* 481-488.

[129] Kirkpatrick, *Ruck it Up,* 485.

[130] Peter W. Rose, II, "American Armor in Albania, A Soldier's Mosaic," *Armor* 108, no. 4 (July-August 1999): 9; Kirkpatrick, *Ruck it Up,* 487-488;

[131] For information on the improved living conditions at Tirana-Rinas, see Rose, II, "American Armor in Albania, A Soldier's Mosaic," 9, 50. For information on the task organization and FMC date of TF Hawk, see Nardulli, et al., *Disjointed War,* 74; Kirkpatrick,

In the final days of April, TF Hawk worked to establish the security conditions that would enable them to begin supporting the U.S. Air Force campaign in Kosovo. The two infantry battalion task forces, 1-6 IN and 2nd Brigade, 505th Parachute Infantry Regiment (2-505 PIR), "[created] a perimeter for basic security and then [maintained] regular reconnaissance patrols outside that perimeter and as far as the high ground around the airport."[132] For additional security, Hendrix deployed teams of tanks and BFVs to blocking positions along the major avenues of approach to the airfield. Next, Hendrix established a forward operating base (FOB) near the Albania-Kosovo border from which TF Hawk conducted mounted patrols, artillery raids and Suppression of Enemy Air Defense (SEAD) missions against Serbian forces operating in the porous border region.[133] During each of these missions, soldiers wore a Kevlar helmet, protective vest, and carried their weapon and basic load of ammunition and water.[134]

In the skies above these ground defensive operations, the aviation element of TF Hawk conducted regular training missions in preparation for a possible deep attack against fielded Serbian forces in Kosovo. Unfortunately, the combination of Serbian low-level air defenses,

---

Ruck it Up, 513; R. Cody Phillips, *Operation JOINT GUARDIAN,* 15.

[132] Kirkpatrick, *Ruck it Up,* 498.

[133] Kirkpatrick, *Ruck it Up,* 498, 500; Rose, II, "American Armor in Albania, A Soldier's Mosaic," 51; Randall K. Cheeseborough, "Multiple Launch Rocket System (MLRS) Deep Fires," *Joint Center for Lessons Learned Bulletin* 2, no. 2 (June 2000): 19, 22.

[134] Detailed packing lists for units deployed in support of Operation Allied Force could not be located. However, photographic evidence in Rose, II, "American Armor in Albania, A Soldier's Mosaic," 9, 50 shows that soldiers executing missions outside the perimeters of Tirana-Rinas or the FOB carried the standard combat fighting load identified in Appendix B, Equipment Weights and Load Calculations. Of note, separate photographic evidence indicates that soldiers did not wear or carry this gear while in the perimeter of Tirana-Rinas or the FOB. While in these secure areas, soldiers carried only their personal weapon and one magazine (~15 lbs. of weight). See: Angela Stafford, "U.S. Air Force Senior Airman Darren Hooper directs an aircraft landing at Rinas Airport, Tiranë, Albania, during NATO Operation Allied Force on April 29, 1999," April 29, 1999, http://www.defense.gov/photos/newsphoto.aspx?newsphotoid=2083 (accessed March 18, 2013).

unfavorable terrain, and pilot inexperience quickly proved such an operation to be much more challenging than originally anticipated. TF Hawk confirmed the risk associated with these missions on May 1, when the crash of an Apache helicopter during a mission rehearsal exercise resulted in the first and only fatalities of Operation Allied Force.[135] The aviators of TF Hawk suffered a second operational blow on May 13, when DOD further the restricted the aerial rules of engagement (ROE) within Kosovo.[136] Unable to overcome these limitations, TF Hawk remained uncommitted for the duration of Operation Allied Force.[137]

After 78 days of non-stop aerial bombardment, Operation Allied Force formally ended on June 9, 1999 when Serbian President Slobodan Milosevic agreed to allow a NATO peacekeeping force, known as Kosovo Force (KFOR), to assume military control of Kosovo.[138] On June 10, the United Nations (UN) codified this agreement in United Nations Security Council Resolution 1244, which tasked KFOR to maintain and enforce the Kosovo-Serbian ceasefire, demilitarize

---

[135] Kirkpatrick, *Ruck it Up,* 500-504; Nardulli, et al., *Disjointed War,* 80-86; Stewart, ed., *American Military History Volume II,* 448. Of note, the fatal Apache crash was the second of two aircraft accidents to occur during Operation Allied Force. The first occurred on April 26, but did not result in any casualties. Additionally, as these deaths were accidental, the U.S. DOD maintains, "Operation ALLIED FORCE was conducted without a single combat fatality." Quote taken from U.S. Department of Defense, *Report to Congress: Kosovo/Operation ALLIED FORCE After Action Report,* xxi.

[136] Clark, *Waging Modern War,* 304-305.

[137] Nardulli, et al., *Disjointed War,* 94-95; Kirkpatrick, *Ruck it Up,* 412-514. Despite its lack of direct, kinetic involvement in Operation Allied Force, many historians believe the sheer presence of TF Hawk along the Albania-Kosovo border likely hastened the capitulation of Serbian forces in June 1999. For a discussion of this argument, see Phillips, *Operation JOINT GUARDIAN,* 16; Nardulli, et al., *Disjointed War,* 95.

[138] North Atlantic Treaty Organization, *Military Technical Agreement Between the International Security Force ("KFOR") and the Governments of the Federal Republic of Yugoslavia and the Republic of Serbia,* http://www.nato.int/koSovo/docu/a990609a.htm (accessed March 18, 2013).

Kosovo liberation groups, and establish a safe and secure environment within Kosovo.[139] In support of this new mission set, the U.S. Army disbanded TF Hawk and deployed fresh troops to Kosovo under the auspices of Operation Joint Guardian.[140] Organized as TF Falcon, the newly arrived U.S. forces consisted two dismounted infantry battalion TFs, one armor battalion TF, one field artillery battalion TF, and one aviation TF.

Almost immediately, TF Falcon became immersed in a flood of retributive violence enacted by ethnic Albanians against Kosovo's Serbian population. U.S. soldiers conducted near continuous mounted patrols throughout their assigned AO, in an attempt to "fight fires, disperse crowds, and quell violence."[141] Day after day, they cleared land mines, destroyed weapons caches, and intervened in armed conflicts between ethnic groups. While not often the intended target of violence, TF Falcon nonetheless reported "40 hostile-fire incidents, 11 mortar attacks, 3 hand grenade attacks, 3 mine strikes, and 7 riots" during their first four months in Kosovo.[142] As a result, commanders continued to require their soldiers to carry a standard combat fighting load

---

[139] United Nations Security Council, United Nations Security Council Resolution 1244, "Kosovo," June 10, 1999, http://daccess-dds-ny.un.org/doc/UNDOC/GEN/N99/172/89/PDF/N9917289.pdf?OpenElement (accessed March 18, 1999).

[140] The mission given to troops deploying in support of Operation Joint Guardian did not qualitatively differ from that of KFOR. For further information on the mission and forces deployed in support of Operation Joint Guardian, see Phillips, *Operation JOINT GUARDIAN*, 16-18, 19; Kirkpatrick, *Ruck it Up*, 512-520; Terrence M. Wallace and Everett A. Johnson, "Positively Focused and Fully Engaged: Lessons from Task Force FALCON," *Joint Center for Lessons Learned Bulletin* 2, no. 2 (June 2000): 30.

[141] Phillips, *Operation JOINT GUARDIAN*, 21-25. For additional information on the routine operations of TF Falcon, see also: Wallace and Johnson, "Positively Focused and Fully Engaged," 33; Timothy R. Reese, Kevin W. Farrell, and Matthew P. Moore, "An Armor Battalion in Kosovo," *Armor* 108, no. 6 (November-December 1999): 26-29.

[142] Phillips, *Operation JOINT GUARDIAN*, 36-37.

when operating outside their base camp.[143] These protective measures served TF Falcon well, as they reported only 25 soldiers WIA and none KIA during this time period. By December 1999, the post-war surge in violence had declined to such an extent that U.S. forces were able to increasingly focus their efforts on the rebuilding Kosovo's war-torn cities and providing humanitarian aid to returning refugees.[144]

As the security situation improved, so too did the living conditions for U.S. Soldiers. In less than four months, civilian contractors turned an empty wheat field in eastern Kosovo into a modern, secure military installation able to house the vast majority of U.S. soldiers deployed in support of Operation Joint Guardian. Named for a Vietnam-era Medal of Honor recipient, Camp Bondsteel sprawled for over three kilometers in any direction and boasted hardstand buildings, showers, and latrines, as well as a post exchange, multiple dining and laundry facilities, a fitness center, chapel, and movie theater.[145] Outside of Camp Bondsteel, soldiers lived in converted military bases, "factories, hotels, and old government buildings" scattered across the TF Falcon

---

[143] Larry Wentz, "The Kosovo Environment," in *Lessons from Kosovo: The KFOR Experience,* ed. Larry Wentz (Washington D.C.: DOD Command and Control Research Program, 2002), 362; Daniel Ernst, "U.S. Army 1st Lt. James Perrine (right) escorts a Serbian citizen from his home in Zitinje, Kosovo," July 26, 1999, http://www.defense.gov/photos/newsphoto.aspx?newsphotoid=2410 (accessed March 18, 2013); Sean A. Terry, "Soldiers of the 504th Parachute Infantry Regiment Maintain Crowd Control," January 9, 2000, http://www.defense.gov/photos/newsphoto.aspx?newsphotoid=2637 (accessed March 18, 2013).

[144] Phillips, *Operation JOINT GUARDIAN,* 28-29, 37; Wallace and Johnson, "Positively Focused and Fully Engaged," 32-33. For information on the type and frequency of KFOR missions for the duration of Operation Joint Guardian, see North Atlantic Treaty Organization, "KFOR Press Statements and News Conferences," http://www.nato.int/kosovo/jnt-grdn.htm (accessed March 18, 2013).

[145] Larry Wentz, "Peacekeeper Quality of Life," in *Lessons from Kosovo: The KFOR Experience,* ed. Larry Wentz (Washington D.C.: DOD Command and Control Research Program, 2002), 385-389; David Perera, "Camp Bondsteel: They Call it 'Little America,'" *Defense Standard* (Fall 2008), http://www.davidperera.com/Perera_DefStan_Camp%20Bondsteel.pdf (accessed March 18, 2013); Phillips, *Operation JOINT GUARDIAN,* 50-51.

AO. The most spartan accommodations were the tents of Outpost SAPPER.[146] These satellite facilities offered only a fraction of the amenities available on Camp Bondsteel; however, in all cases, they provided soldiers protection from the elements, hygiene facilities, limited entertainment opportunities, and a modicum of privacy.[147]

In December 1999, the U.S. Army executed its first troop rotation in support of Operation Joint Guardian.[148] New units transitioned easily "into their peace-enforcement mission," and violence continued to decrease throughout the country.[149] After this inaugural rotation, U.S. Army units rotated through Kosovo at six- to nine-month intervals in accordance with DOD guidance. However, the dramatic reduction in violence after 1999, coupled with the onset of Operations Enduring Freedom and Iraqi Freedom, resulted in quantitative and qualitative changes to the U.S. Army's contribution to KFOR from 2003-2012. Specifically, Presidential "Letters to Congressional Leaders Reporting on Deployments of United States Combat-Equipped Armed Forces Around the World" catalogue the reduction of the U.S. Army KFOR contingent from 2,250 active duty soldiers in 2003 to 817 U.S. Army National Guard soldiers in 2012.[150] Changes

---

[146] Wentz, *Lessons from Kosovo*, 384; Michael Scott, "A Taste of Life at Outpost SAPPER: Supporting Peace on a Volatile Border," *Armor* 111, no. 3 (May-June 2001): 11.

[147] Scott, "A Taste of Life at Outpost SAPPER," 11-12.

[148] Phillips, *Operation JOINT GUARDIAN*, 37. Following this inaugural rotation, units have continued to rotate through Kosovo at six- to nine-month intervals in accordance with DOD guidance. The American Forces Press Service covers the rotation of U.S. Army units to and from Kosovo; their coverage can be found at *U.S. Department of Defense*, s.v. "KFOR," https://www.defense.gov (accessed March 18, 2013).

[149] Phillips, *Operation JOINT GUARDIAN*, 37, 50. For examples of routine missions conducted by U.S. Army units in Kosovo during this period, see Neal Mayo and Bryan Collins, interview by Barbra Klein, *All Things Considered*, NPR, June 18, 2000; Lee A. Flemming, "The Way Ahead: Lessons from Gnjilane, Kosovo," *Infantry* 91, no. 1 (Spring 2002): 28-31; Erik Krivda and Kamil Sztalkoper, "Conducting Vehicle Checkpoints in Kosovo," *Infantry* 92, no. 2 (Winter 2003): 16-18.

[150] For information on the number and mission of U.S. forces assigned to KFOR from the

years 1999-2012, see: George W. Bush, "Letter to Congressional Leaders Reporting on the Deployment of United States Military Personnel as Part of the Kosovo International Security Force," *Weekly Compilation of Presidential Documents* (June 12, 1999); George W. Bush, "Letter to Congressional Leaders Reporting on the Deployment of United States Military Personnel as Part of the Kosovo International Security Force," *Weekly Compilation of Presidential Documents* (June 16, 2000); George W. Bush, "Letter to Congressional Leaders Reporting on the Deployment of United States Military Personnel as Part of the Kosovo International Security Force," *Weekly Compilation of Presidential Documents* (May 18, 2001); George W. Bush, "Letter to Congressional Leaders Reporting on the Deployment of United States Military Personnel as Part of the Kosovo International Security Force," *Weekly Compilation of Presidential Documents* (May 14, 2003); George W. Bush, "Letter to Congressional Leaders Reporting on Deployment of United States Combat-Equipped Armed Forces Around the World," *Weekly Compilation of Presidential Documents* (May 20, 2005); George W. Bush, "Letter to Congressional Leaders Reporting on Deployments of United States Combat-Equipped Armed Forces Around the World," *Weekly Compilation of Presidential Documents* (June 15, 2006); George W. Bush, "Letter to Congressional Leaders Reporting on Deployments of United States Combat-Equipped Armed Forces Around the World," *Weekly Compilation of Presidential Documents* (June 15, 2007); George W. Bush, "Letter to Congressional Leaders Reporting on the Deployments of United States Combat-Equipped Armed Forces Around the World," *Weekly Compilation of Presidential Documents* (June 13, 2008); Barack Obama, "Letter to Congressional Leaders on the Global Deployments of United States Combat-Equipped Armed Forces," *Weekly Compilation of Presidential Documents* (June 15, 2009); Barack Obama, "Letter to Congressional Leaders on the Global Deployments of United States Combat-Equipped Armed Forces," *Weekly Compilation of Presidential Documents* (June 15, 2010); Barack Obama, "Letter to Congressional Leaders on the Global Deployments of United States Combat-Equipped Armed Forces," *Weekly Compilation of Presidential Documents* (June 15, 2011); Barack Obama, "Letter to Congressional Leaders on the Deployment of United States Combat-Equipped Armed Forces," *Weekly Compilation of Presidential Documents* (June 15, 2012). For information on the specific units deployed in support of KFOR rotations, see: Linda D. Kozaryn, "Life as a U.S. Peacekeeper in Kosovo," *Defense.gov*, December 27, 1999, http://www.defense.gov/news/newsarticle.aspx?id=42907 (accessed March 19, 2013); Linda D. Kozaryn, "SHAPE Considers Troop Needs for Kosovo Force," *Defense.gov*, April 6, 2000, http://www.defense.gov/news/newsarticle.aspx?id=45087 (accessed March 19, 2013); Roxana Tiron, "NATO Units in Kosovo Predict Mission Could Last a Decade," *NationalDefense Magazine.org,* March 2003, http://www.nationaldefensemagazine.org/archive/2003/March/Pages/NATO_Units3922.aspx (accessed March 19, 2013); Pennsylvania Army National Guard, "KFOR 5A – Pennsylvania Army National Guard," Windows Media Player video file, 1:07.55, http://www.youtube.com/watch?v=2tTEuwjZQrw (accessed March 19, 2013); Terri Lukach, "Kosovo Mission Successful, Important, U.S. Forces Say," *Defense.gov*, August 15, 2005, http://www.defense.gov/news/newsarticle.aspx?id=16883 (accessed March 19, 2013); Donna Miles, "Kosovo Force Prepares for Political Status Resolution," *Defense.gov,* November 15, 2006, http://www.defense.gov/news/newsarticle.aspx?id=2125 (accessed March 19, 2013); Jim Greenhill, "National Guard's Critical Role in Kosovo," *NG.mil*, May 25, 2007, http://www.ng.mil/news/archives/2007/05/052507-kosovo.aspx (accessed March 19, 2013); Lindsey M. Frazier, "Face of Defense: Mother, Son Prepare to Deploy to Kosovo Together," *Defense.gov*, May 15, 2008, http://www.defense.gov/News/NewsArticle.aspx?ID=49881

to the security environment and force structure also impacted the nature and frequency of KFOR missions. As compared to the experiences of TF Falcon in 1999, soldiers deployed during this time period routinely conducted fewer security patrols, fewer checkpoints, and fewer offensive operations. The scarcity of enemy activity also prompted many commanders to reduce force protection levels and allow soldiers conducting routine missions to operate without body armor or Kevlar helmets.[151] The relative security and stability experienced by these soldiers ultimately persisted for ninety-six percent of Operation Joint Guardian.[152]

From strategic resistance to the introduction of ground troops, to operational insistence on the exclusivity of the air campaign, to widespread tactical use of mounted patrols once in Kosovo—Operations Allied Force and Joint Guardian clearly demonstrate the U.S. Army's increasing desire to leverage advanced technological platforms to improve both the survivability and lethality of its soldiers.[153] The success of these tactics is evidenced by the complete absence

---

(accessed March 19, 2013); Michael Hagburg, "Kosovo Force to Transform into Deterrent Presence," *Defense.gov*, January 5, 2010, http://www.defense.gov/news/newsarticle.aspx?id=57362 (accessed March 19, 2013); Jerry Boffen, "KFOR 12 Commander Holds Final Meeting with Kosovo Media," *NG.mil*, July 9, 2010, http://www.ng.mil/news/archives/2010/07/070910-KFOR.aspx (accessed March 19, 2013); Donna Miles, "U.S. Commander Condemns Attacks on Kosovo Force," *Defense.gov*, November 29, 2011, http://www.defense.gov/news/newsarticle.aspx?id=66279 (accessed March 19, 2013); Donna Miles, "Kosovo Force Rotation Prepares for Peacekeeping Mission," *Defense.gov*, August 31, 2012, http://www.defense.gov/News/NewsArticle.aspx?ID=117702 (accessed March 19, 2013); Steven Beardsley, "Active-duty Troops to Deploy to Kosovo for First Time in a Decade," *Stripes.com*, March 13, 2013, http://www.stripes.com/news/active-duty-troops-to-deploy-to-kosovo-for-first-time-in-a-decade-1.211663 (accessed March 19, 2013).

[151] Phillips, *Operation JOINT GUARDIAN,* 50.

[152] By all accounts, TF Falcon's rotation to Kosovo was the most arduous and lethal. This accounts for six months, or roughly 4%, of the 150 total months of Operation Joint Guardian that occurred during the period analyzed.

[153] Clark, *Waging Modern War,* 304-305, 320-321, 367. This concern was also reflected at the strategic level, see: William J. Clinton, "Statement on Kosovo;" William J. Clinton, interview by Dan Rather, *CBS News*, CBS, March 31, 1999; Kenneth Bacon, "U.S. Department of Defense News Briefing, March 23, 1999."

of combat-related fatalities in either conflict.[154] Furthermore, the U.S. Army's ability and

willingness to quickly improve quality of life for deployed soldiers indicates an inclination to

address the concerns of the Presidential Commission regarding the austerity and difficulty of

combat. Overall, these factors support the contention that revoking the gendered combat

exclusion policy poses a low operational risk to the success of U.S. Army operations.

Operation Enduring Freedom, Afghanistan

Over the course of 102 minutes on September 11, 2001, nineteen terrorists changed the

lives of American citizens forever. Acting on the orders of Usama bin Ladin (UBL), leader of the

radical Islamist group al-Qaeda (AQ), these men hijacked and purposely crashed commercial

airliners into three separate sites along the eastern seaboard of the United States. Their actions

resulted in the death of 2,973 innocent civilians—the single largest non-combatant loss of life

from hostile action on American soil in the nation's history.[155] On September 12, still reeling

from the shock and intensity of the attacks, President George W. Bush ordered his National

Security Council to "develop a strategy to eliminate terrorists and punish those who support

---

[154] The Defense Manpower Data Center does not maintain data on Operation Joint Guardian; however, an examination of their database shows zero U.S. Army deaths from hostile action from 1999-2000. The year 2001—the same year OEF began—is the first time combat-related fatalities re-appear in the overall numbers of U.S. Army deaths. See Defense Manpower Data Center, "Active Duty Military Deaths by Year and Manner (1980-2010)," Defense Casualty Analysis System, https://www.dmdc.osd.mil/dcas/pages/report_by_year_manner.xhtml (accessed March 25, 2013). The Defense Manpower Data Center also does not maintain data on WIA or POW for Operation Joint Guardian. Phillips states that 25 soldiers were WIA in combat related incidents in 1999 and three soldiers taken POW from Macedonia in an incident that occurred during, but not in relation to, the Allied Force campaign. See Phillips, *Operation JOINT GUARDIAN,* 14, 39, 49.

[155] United States, National Commission on Terrorist Attacks Upon the United States, *The 9/11 Commission Report* (Washington D.C.: Government Printing Office, 2004), xv, 47-70, 285, 311.

them."[156] Three weeks later, during an emotional address to a joint session of Congress, Bush confirmed the culpability of AQ in the September 11 attacks and announced his intent to use "all elements of national power" to not only "eliminate the AQ network," but to find and defeat "every terrorist group of global reach."[157] With these words, America embarked what would become known as the Global War on Terror (GWOT). In the decade following this announcement, the U.S. Army deployed soldiers to over 53 nations in support of the overall GWOT.[158] The first of these operations, and one of only two campaigns currently recognized by the U.S. Army CMH during this period, was Operation Enduring Freedom.[159]

General Tommy Franks, the USCENTCOM commander from 2000-2003, quickly identified the small, landlocked country of Afghanistan as the first battlefield in the GWOT. Franks based his decision on years of intelligence reporting that indicated Afghanistan's ruling party, the Taliban, had repeatedly and voluntarily provided sanctuary to AQ operatives. The Taliban's refusal to sever their ties with AQ in the aftermath of 9/11 further supported Franks'

---

[156] National Commission on Terrorist Attacks Upon the United States, *The 9/11 Commission Report*, 330-331; George W. Bush, "Address to the Nation on the Terrorist Attacks," *Public Papers of the Presidents of the United States* (September 11, 2001), http://www.presidency.ucsb.edu/ws/index.php?pid=58057 (accessed March 19, 2013).

[157] George W. Bush, "Address to a Joint Session of Congress and the American People," *Public Papers of the Presidents of the United States* (September 20, 2001), http://georgewbush-whitehouse.archives.gov/news/releases/2001/09/20010920-8.html (accessed March 19, 2013); *Testimony of U.S. Secretary of Defense Donald H. Rumsfeld Before The National Commission on Terrorist Attacks Upon the United States*, (March 23, 2004) (prepared statement of Donald H. Rumsfeld, U.S. Secretary of Defense), 7.

[158] U.S. Army Human Resources Command Awards and Decorations Branch, "Global War on Terrorism Expeditionary Medal GWOTEM and Global War on Terrorism Service Medal GWOTSM," U.S. Army Human Resources Command, https://www.hrc.army.mil/TAGD/Global%20War%20on%20Terrorism%20Expeditionary%20Medal%20GWOTEM%20and%20Global%20War%20on%20Terrorism%20Service%20Medal%20GWOTSM (accessed March 22, 2013).

[159] U.S. Army CMH, "Campaigns of the U.S. Army," U.S. Army CMH, http://www.history.army.mil/html/reference/campaigns.html (accessed March 22, 2012).

analysis and provided diplomatic justification for military action.[160] However, "like the unconventional attack that provoked it," the American intervention in Afghanistan quickly proved to be a "different kind of war."[161] Most significantly, in an effort to "signal [American] determination without provoking Afghan concerns about foreign intervention," USCENTCOM planners chose from the outset to employ a combination of SOF teams and aerial strike and bomber platforms rather than large numbers of conventional forces.[162] According to Franks, this force package provided the best method for the United States to quickly and efficiently "destroy AQ in Afghanistan and remove the Taliban from power."[163] Ten days after the 9/11 attacks, the Bush Administration approved Franks' plan, now code-named Operation Enduring Freedom (OEF), and authorized USCENTCOM to deploy the personnel and equipment necessary for the execution of the campaign.[164]

---

[160] Specifically, in his address before the joint session of Congress on September 20, 2001, Bush stated that "any nation that continues to harbor or support terrorism [would] be regarded by the United States as a hostile regime." The international community supported Bush's stance, as evidenced by UN Resolutions 1269 and 1368, UNSCR 1373, NATO's invocation of Article V of the NATO treaty, the invocation of the Inter-American Treaty of Reciprocal Assistance among the Organization of American States (OAS), and Australia's invocation of the ANZUS treaty. For further, see: Bush, "Address to a Joint Session of Congress and the American People," (September 20, 2001); Donald P. Wright, *A Different Kind of War: The United States Army in Operation ENDURING FREEDOM, October 2001-September 2005* (Fort Leavenworth, KS: Combat Studies Institute Press, 2010), 27. For a complete discussion of the evolution of the AQ-Taliban relationship, see National Commission on Terrorist Attacks Upon the United States, *The 9/11 Commission Report*.

[161] Wright, *A Different Kind of War*, 1.

[162] Tommy R. Franks, *American Soldier* (New York, NY: HarperCollins, 2004), 271; Wright, *A Different Kind of War*, 45.

[163] Franks, *American Soldier*, 252; Wright, *A Different Kind of War*, 45.

[164] The original code-name for OEF, Operation Infinite Justice, was amended by the Bush Administration after concerns regarding its religious connotations were brought to light by the American-Muslim population. See Wright, *A Different Kind of War*, 27, 45-46.

U.S. Army support to combat operations in Afghanistan began with the infiltration of multiple SOF teams, called Operational Detachment-Alphas (ODA), across the mountainous borders of Afghanistan. From October 19 to November 8, 2001, MH-47 Chinook helicopters flew eight separate missions, dropping teams of six to twelve soldiers into remote Afghan landing zones where they joined forces with members of anti-Taliban militia groups.[165] Uncertain how long they would be in the country, each member of the ODA reportedly carried several days worth of rations and ammunition in addition to their standard combat load. No specific information regarding the exact ODA packing list could be located; however, during a television interview one year after the invasion, a member of ODA 595 identified only as a Master Sergeant Paul recounted that his team "all had very heavy packs…just around a hundred pounds worth of equipment, and a couple of extra bags."[166] Once on the ground, the ODAs embedded themselves entirely with their assigned militia counterpart. They slept in cattle stables, mud huts, or caves; they traveled entirely by horse or truck—side by side with the Afghans.[167]

---

[165] Wright, *A Different Kind of War*, 71-105; Richard W. Stewart, *Operation ENDURING FREEDOM: The United States Army in Afghanistan, October 2001 – March 2002* (Washington, D.C.: Center of Military History, 2004), 10. Of note, the air campaign in support of OEF began on October 7, 2001, twelve days prior to the arrival of the first ground troops in Afghanistan. For details on this portion of the campaign, see Wright, *A Different Kind of War*, 62-64.

[166] The standard combat load for a SOF soldier is similar to the standard combat load identified in Appendix B. Despite photographic evidence indicating that (a) SOF soldiers occasionally opted not to wear their issued combat uniforms [BDU, DCU, or Advanced Combat Uniform (ACU)] in favor of various civilian equivalents, and (b) SOF soldiers did not don their protective gear as routinely as conventional soldiers it is unlikely that either of these alterations significantly or permanently lightened the combat load of the average SOF soldier during OEF. Furthermore, evidence indicates that due to the forward deployed nature of ODA operations in support of OEF, ODA members often carried additional rations. Specific reporting indicates that at least one ODA routinely carried two additional MREs and five additional quarts of water; the weight of these rations is 15.5 lbs. and brings the standard combat load for an ODA soldier to 100.5 lbs. See: Stewart, *Operation ENDURING FREEDOM*, 12; ODA 595, unidentified interviewer, *Frontline*, PBS, August 2, 2002.

[167] ODA 595, unidentified interviewer, *Frontline*, PBS, August 2, 2002; ODA 555, unidentified interviewer, *Frontline*, PBS, August 2, 2002; Wright, *A Different Kind of War*, 76-

More than simply demonstrating solidarity with the anti-Taliban cause, the ODAs quickly

demonstrated their operational importance on the battlefield. At every opportunity they used

"laser illuminators and Global Positioning System (GPS) equipment" to direct "precision-guided

airstrikes in support of an indigenous ally against enemy forces."[168] The tactic, which became

known as ground-directed interdiction (GDI), enabled the ODAs to target and destroy Taliban

and AQ formations while still well beyond the effective range of the enemy's weapons systems.

In essence, GDI "enabled the concentration of devastating effects without concentrating physical

forces," which allowed "US forces [to achieve] maximum effectiveness with minimal risk."[169]

When combined with an effective ground force, the efforts of the ODAs were overwhelmingly

lethal; however, cultural differences periodically derailed even the most promising of operations.

The most significant example of this misfortune was the escape of UBL from Tora Bora, a

Taliban stronghold in the mountains of eastern Afghanistan. During the incident, a key Afghan

militia leader abandoned his assigned ODA in favor of breaking his Ramadan-imposed fast in the

safety of his own lines.[170] Despite periodic setbacks, the impact of "SOF-directed US air power"

and ODA mentorship enabled the disparate elements of the anti-Taliban militia to seize control of

the country in less than eight weeks.[171]

77; 101-104.

[168] Wright, *A Different Kind of War*, 86. For additional information on the missions and experiences of ODAs during OEF, see also "The Liberation of Mazar-e Sharif: 5th SF Group Conducts UW in Afghanistan," *Special Warfare* 15, no. 2 (June 2002): 34-41.

[169] Wright, *A Different Kind of War*, 86.

[170] Wright, *A Different Kind of War*, 80, 113-120.

[171] Of note, elements of the Northern Alliance (NA) seized the major population centers of Mazar-e Sharif, Taloqan, and Konduz; while elements loosely organized under the Eastern Alliance (EA) seized Tarin Kowt, Bagram, and Kabul, and Kandahar. See Wright, *A Different Kind of War*, 88, 93.

Building upon the incredible success of the ODA operations, U.S. forces (USF) in

Afghanistan moved into the second major phase of OEF—deliberate combat operations—in

March of 2002. USCENTCOM supported this transition by funneling additional combat power to

Afghanistan. Over the next fourteen months, the U.S. Army rotated two Combined Joint Task

Force (CJTF) headquarters elements and three infantry brigade task forces (TF) through

Afghanistan at six-month intervals.[172] From the spring of 2002 to the spring of 2003, these units

conducted a total of eleven major security operations, each aimed at establishing a safe and secure

environment for Afghanistan's first post-war loya jirga.[173] The first of these operations, code

named Anaconda, occurred over a three week period in early March 2002; the second to last

operation, code named Valiant Strike, took place over 72-hours in April 2003. The scope,

duration, and conduct of these missions provide excellent examples of the character of warfare

experienced by soldiers during this phase of OEF.[174]

TF Rakkasan, the first conventional combat forces to arrive in Afghanistan after the

initial invasion, executed Operation Anaconda from March 1 – 19, 2002. With the assistance of

five ODAs and two Afghan militia elements, TF Rakkasan conducted multiple attacks on large

---

[172] USCENTCOM arranged this deployment schedule based on U.S. Army's experiences in the Balkans. The elements deployed included: CJTF Mountain (10th Mountain Division), CJTF 180 (82d Airborne Division), TF Rakkasan (3-101AASLT), TF Panther (3/82ABN), and TF Devil (1/82ABN). See Wright, *A Different Kind of War*, 127-218 for specific information on the composition and missions of these TFs.

[173] Loya jirga is the Pashto phrase for grand council. A loya jirga is a gathering of elders and civic leaders where matters of state are discussed and decided. For further, see BBC News, "What is a Loya Jirga?" *BBCNews.com*, July 1, 2002, http://news.bbc.co.uk/2/hi/south_asia/1782079.stm (accessed March 22, 2013).

[174] Operations conducted under the purview of CJTF Mountain and CJTF-180 from March 2002-July 2003 include: Operations Anaconda, Mountain Lion, Mountain Sweep, Village Search, Champion Strike, Mongoose, Viper, Valiant Strike, Resolute Strike, Unified Venture, and Deliberate Strike. See Wright, *A Different Kind of War*, 184-189, 212-218; Marie Schult, "Operation Valiant Strike," *Army* 53, no. 5 (May 2003): 59-60.

concentrations of AQ and Taliban forces operating within the Shahi Kowt Valley of southern Afghanistan.[175] While ultimately viewed as a success by the U.S. Army, Operation Anaconda exposed several significant limitations associated with the employment of ground forces in direct combat operations in Afghanistan. Most notably, TF Rakkasan quickly discovered that they had underestimated the challenge Afghanistan's rugged terrain posed to their operations. For example, troops inserted by CH-47 Chinook helicopters found they still might have another "2,000-foot climb at altitudes of over 8,000 feet" to complete their mission; those traveling by vehicle found that a recent snowfall had turned the "dirt roads into mushy, slippery quagmires that significantly slowed movement through terrain that was difficult to negotiate in daylight."[176] To further complicate matters, soldiers executed their missions carrying equipment weighing anywhere from 85 to 90 pounds.[177] When in contact with the enemy, soldiers lightened their loads

---

[175] *Operation Anaconda Combat Operations Brief* (brief, CJTF Mountain, February 26, 2002). For a complete account of Operation Anaconda, see Wright, *A Different Kind of War*, 127-174.

[176] Wright, *A Different Kind of War*, 141, 143-146, 159; P. McGuire, "Task Force Rakkasan: 3-101st, Aviation Regiment 03/02-08/02," in *Long Hard Road: NCO Experiences in Afghanistan and Iraq*, ed. L.R. Arms (Fort Bliss, TX: U.S. Army Sergeants Major Academy, 2007), 19.

[177] The most comprehensive collection of data regarding the modern soldier combat load can be found in Task Force Devil CAAT, *The Modern Warrior's Combat Load*. Conducted from April-May 2003, the study provides detailed information on the experiences of an infantry brigade task force conducting security operations in eastern Afghanistan. Data contained within *The Modern Warrior's Combat Load* provides the foundation for many of the calculations in this study; specifically, a modified version of the infantry rifleman packing list was used as the basis of the standard soldier combat load. Modifications were made based on the preponderance of equipment and weight data gleaned from all case studies and resulted in a discrepancy of roughly 6 lbs. between the standard soldier combat load depicted in Appendix B and infantry rifleman data presented in *The Modern Warrior's Combat Load*. For further, see Task Force Devil CAAT, *The Modern Warrior's Combat Load*, 17-19.

by discarding their assault packs; however, the 55-60 lbs. of gear they still carried significantly slowed their progress on the daunting upward slopes of the Afghan mountains.[178]

Despite these challenges, U.S. Army troops found that the tactics pioneered by the ODA and Afghan militias during the first phase of OEF remained incredibly effective in destroying enemy formations. At every opportunity, TF Rakkasan incorporated close combat attack (CCA) support from the division's AH-64 Apache helicopters and close air support (CAS) from U.S. Air Force fixed wing assets into their attacks on AQ and Taliban elements. The mobility and vantage point of these aerial platforms, combined with the incredible firepower of their onboard weapons systems, provided U.S. ground forces with an overwhelming advantage against the lightly armed enemy force. In fact, CAS and GDI tactics were so effective that USF reportedly killed over 100 enemy fighters for every one American soldier KIA during Operation Anaconda.[179] This operation clearly capitalized on the successes of the initial invasion and thus contributed to maintaining the initiative for USF operating in Afghanistan. However, it also proved to be incredibly manpower and resource intensive. This fact, complicated further by the onset war in

---

[178] For example, the unit required to make the 2,000-foot ascent described earlier in this paragraph likely only wore a fighting load of 52.49 lbs., however they still required four hours to summit and secure Takur Ghar (their objective). For the details of this maneuver, see Wright, *A Different Kind of War*, 158-159. For additional evidence detailing the standard combat loads carried by soldiers during this phase of OEF, see: Wright, *A Different Kind of War*, 133, 146, 149, 155; Task Force Devil CAAT, *The Modern Warrior's Combat Load;* C. Peterson, "Baptism by Fire: 705th Ordnance Company, Afghanistan 10/02-06/03," in *Long Hard Road: NCO Experiences in Afghanistan and Iraq*, ed. L. R. Arms (Fort Bliss, TX: U.S. Army Sergeants Major Academy, 2007), 29. For evidence confirming the discarding of extra weight during firefights, see Wright, *A Different Kind of War*, 153, 155.

[179] CJTF Mountain reported eight soldiers KIA and forty WIA during Operation Anaconda. See *Afghanistan and Operation ANACONDA* (brief, CJTF Mountain, n.d.); "Operation Anaconda Costs 8 U.S. Lives," *CNN World*, March 4, 2002, http://articles.cnn.com/2002-03-04/world/ret.afghan.fighting_1_shahi-kot-afghan-forces-qaeda-and-taliban?_s=PM:asiapcf (accessed March 23, 2013); Wright, *A Different Kind of War,* 173; McGuire, "Task Force Rakkasan," in *Long Hard Road*, 19.

Iraq, forced security operations in Afghanistan to dwindle in size and duration over the course of the next twelve months.

The clearest example of this reduction is Operation Valiant Strike. Conducted exactly one year after Operation Anaconda, Operation Valiant Strike included only a fraction of the combat power and operational scope of its predecessor. Specifically, the CJTF headquarters employed two infantry battalion TFs, one unit of the newly formed Afghan National Army (ANA), several Civil Affairs (CA) specialists, linguists, and a small contingent of female U.S. Army soldiers to cordon and search a string of villages in the Maruf district of Afghanistan. For three days these soldiers moved on foot through the Sami Ghar Mountains, methodically surrounding, securing, and searching any settlement they encountered. These maneuvers met with no active enemy resistance; however, they did uncover multiple weapons caches. When Operation Valiant Strike ended on March 22, 2003, U.S. troops had seized "50 rifles, two heavy machine guns, 170-mm rockets and 400 82-mm mortar rounds" without suffering a single casualty.[180] Most notably, during Operation Valiant Strike commanders on the ground reported that the contributions of soldiers with non-combat related MOS were likely to be critical in ensuring the durability of these security gains. Specifically, the presence of female soldiers and CA personnel enabled USF to engage previously marginalized portions of the population, which commanders believed would contribute to the development of long-term security solutions throughout Maruf province.[181] These soldiers, uniquely qualified by their gender or non-combat skill sets, established relationships that provided a vital foundation for USF to shift their focus to building the political, economic, and military capacity of the new Afghan nation.[182] In all, the relative success of low-

---

[180] Schult, "Operation Valiant Strike," 59-60.

[181] Wright, *A Different Kind of War*, 217-218.

[182] Franks, *American Soldier*, 271; Wright; *A Different Kind of War*, 237.

54

intensity, short-duration missions such as Operation Valiant Strike effectively punctuated the evolution of decisive combat operations during OEF and prompted USF in Afghanistan to segue into a new phase of the campaign.

Major changes accompanied the U.S. Army's shift from security to stability operations during the final phase of OEF. The most fundamental and far-reaching of these transitions was the introduction of a coordinated counterinsurgency (COIN) campaign plan by the new USCENTCOM headquarters in Afghanistan, Combined Forces Command-Afghanistan (CFC-A). This new strategy was a drastic departure from the combat-centric mentality of the first two phases of the operation. It required units to deliberately decrease tactical operations in favor of increasing support to non-kinetic tasks such as Afghan security force development and infrastructure reconstruction.[183]

To meet these objectives, USCENTCOM increasingly augmented troop requirements for OEF. From 2002 to 2012, the average monthly number of "boots on the ground" (BOG) in Afghanistan rose by a factor of 13—from 5,200 soldiers to a high of 63,500.[184] Increased combat power enabled CFC-A to pursue the first of five pillars in its COIN campaign plan, sustaining area ownership.[185] Specifically, it allowed CFC-A to expand its footprint in Afghanistan beyond

---

[183]The goal of CFC-A Commander LTG David W. Barno was to "focus 80 percent of [CFC-A's] resources on civil affairs and political initiatives and the remaining 20 percent on military actions." Wright, *A Different Kind of War*, 245.

[184] U.S. Library of Congress, Congressional Research Service, *Troop Levels in the Afghan and Iraq Wars, FY2001-FY2012: Cost and Other Potential Issues* by Amy Belasco, (Washington, D.C.: The Service, 2009), 9.

[185] David W. Barno, "Fighting "The Other War:" Counterinsurgency Strategy in Afghanistan, 2003-2005," *Military Review* (September-October 2007): 35. Of note, only three of the five pillars identified in the CFC-A COIN campaign were within the purview of the main combat forces in Afghanistan. CFC-A assigned responsibility for the second pillar, enabling Afghan security structure, to the Office of Military Cooperation-Afghanistan (OMC-A) and maintained responsibility for the fifth pillar, engaging regional states, at the CFC level.

the handful of well-equipped FOBs it operated from during 2001-2003 to hundreds of combat outposts (COP) established near key villages and infiltration routes throughout the Afghan countryside.[186] These small, forward deployed camps created a physical link between U.S. Army units and the citizens in their areas of responsibility (AOR), directly contributing to the creation of a "durable security environment" throughout the country.[187]

In many instances, however, the logistical difficulty of establishing and maintaining these far-flung COPs tempered their utility. For example, 173rd Airborne Infantry Brigade (173rd ABN) soldiers deployed to the Korengal Valley were forced to literally scratch their new homes into the sides of mountains—filling sandbags and multi-cellular defense barriers with rocks chipped from the cliffs surrounding their position.[188] Others such as 1st Battalion, 87th Infantry Regiment (1-87IN); 2nd Battalion, 2nd Infantry Regiment (2-2IN); and 2nd Battalion, 5th Infantry Regiment (2-5IN) occupied mud huts, set up U.S. Army issue tents, or built small wooden structures from which to conduct their operations.[189] All had limited access to electricity and hygiene facilities,

---

[186] U.S. Library of Congress, Congressional Research Service, *War in Afghanistan: Strategy, Military Operations, and Other Issues for Congress* by Steve Bowman and Catherine Dale, (Washington, D.C.: The Service, 2009), 29. For information on the living conditions at FOBs during OEF, see: C. Peterson, "Baptism by Fire," in *Long Hard Road*, 31; L. Gholston, "Air Medical Evacuation: 68th Medical Company Air Ambulance, Afghanistan 11/03-11/04," in *Long Hard Road: NCO Experiences in Afghanistan and Iraq*, ed. L. R. Arms (Fort Bliss, TX: U.S. Army Sergeants Major Academy, 2007), 38-40.

[187] Wright, *A Different Kind of War*, 246. For a detailed discussion of the evolution of the AOR in OEF, specifically the establishment of Regional Commands and their associated military command structures, see: International Security Assistance Force (ISAF), "History," ISAF, http://www.isaf.nato.int/history.html (accessed March 24, 2013); Ian Hope, "Unity of Command in Afghanistan: A Forsaken Principle of War," (Carlisle paper, U. S., Army War College, November 2008).

[188] Sebastian Junger, *War*, (New York, NY: 12, 2010), 63-64.

[189] Wright, *A Different Kind of War*, 249, 253; D. Berry, "Establishing a Special Forces Firebase: ODA 381, 3rd Bn, 3rd SFG (Airborne)," in *Long Hard Road: NCO Experiences in Afghanistan and Iraq*, ed. L. R. Arms (Fort Bliss, TX: U.S. Army Sergeants Major Academy, 2007), 60; W. Forro, "Building a Forward Operating Base: 2nd Battalion, 5th Infantry Battalion" in

however none could be classified as comfortable.[190] Once established, these COPs survived

largely at the mercy of their supply chain. CH-47 and UH-60 helicopters airlifted pallets of

MREs, water, fuel, and ammunition to the forward deployed units. When possible, they also

delivered additional men and materiel to assist in expanding and improving the site.[191]

Soon, COP occupants began to supplement these deliveries by contracting with local

residents for the supplies and manpower necessary to complete their construction efforts.[192] These

business transactions paved the way for soldiers to support the second pillar of the CFC-A COIN

campaign, enabling reconstruction and good governance.[193] Specifically, soldiers leveraged the

legitimate business opportunities provided by COP construction to establish relationships with

local civic leaders and tribal elders. Units then worked with U.S. Provincial Reconstruction

Teams (PRT) to develop projects specifically designed to improve the quality of life for Afghans

in their AORs; they built wells, refurbished schools, and initiated agricultural projects aimed at

undermining the illicit production of poppy crops. Platoon- to company-sized ground combat

units oversaw these efforts, alternately providing protection and manpower to ensure mission

completion.[194] Over time, the successful execution of these operations created small pockets of

---

Long Hard Road: NCO Experiences in Afghanistan and Iraq, ed. L. R. Arms (Fort Bliss, TX: U.S. Army Sergeants Major Academy, 2007), 68.

[190] Forro, "Building a Forward Operating Base," in *Long Hard Road,* 68; Junger, *War,* 65.

[191] L. Hall, "Make a Way: 725th Main Support Battalion, Afghanistan, 03/04-02/05," in *Long Hard Road: NCO Experiences in Afghanistan and Iraq*, ed. L. R. Arms (Fort Bliss, TX: U.S. Army Sergeants Major Academy, 2007), 42; Forro, "Building a Forward Operating Base," in *Long Hard Road,* 68-69.

[192] Berry, "Establishing a Special Forces Firebase," in *Long Hard Road,* 61-62; Forro, "Building a Forward Operating Base," in *Long Hard Road,* 68-69.

[193] Barno, "Fighting "The Other War,"" 35.

[194] Wright, *A Different Kind of War*, 246-247, 250, 255-261, 293-296; Jerry Meyerle,

stability and progress across Afghanistan, which degraded the base of support for enemy forces

and demonstrating the long-term commitment of the United States to the reconstruction of

Afghanistan.[195]

    CFC-A's reconstruction efforts did not go unchallenged. AQ and Taliban elements

remained a determined and formidable foe throughout the country, most significantly in the

ungoverned spaces along the Afghanistan-Pakistan border region.[196] To counter this threat, USF

conducted security operations in support of the final operational pillar of the CFC-A COIN

campaign plan, defeating terrorism and denying sanctuary to the enemy.[197] Most commonly these

efforts consisted of routine mounted and dismounted patrols that began and ended at a FOB or

COP. The best resourced of these operations used HMMWVs equipped with crew-served

machine guns to maneuver soldiers through the rugged Afghan terrain; more often, the extreme

slope and elevation of the mountains forced soldiers to conduct their missions on foot, armed only

with what weaponry they could carry.[198] These operations placed an immense physical strain on

---

Megan Katt, and Jim Gabrilis, "A US Army Battalion in Kunar and Nuristan, 2007-2008," in *Counterinsurgency on the Ground in Afghanistan: How Different Units Adapted to Local Conditions,* (Washington, D.C.: CNA Strategic Studies, 2010), 51-61; Nathan Springer, "Implementing a Population-Centric Counterinsurgency Strategy: Northeast Afghanistan, May 07-July 08," *Small Wars Journal* (2010); Meyerle, et al., "A US Army Battalion in Khost, 2004-2008," in *Counterinsurgency on the Ground in Afghanistan,* 63-69; Meyerle, et al., "A US Army Battalion in Nangarhar Province, 2005-2009," in *Counterinsurgency on the Ground in Afghanistan,* 71-82; Anthony E. Carlson, "Forging Alliances at Yargul Village: A Lieutenant's Struggle to Improve Security," in *Vanguard of Valor: Small Unit Actions in Afghanistan*, ed. Donald P. Wright (Fort Leavenworth, KS: Combat Studies Institute Press, 2011), 73-87.

[195] Wright, *A Different Kind of War*, 285.

[196] As recently as 2012, Regional Command-East (RC-E), located in the southeastern corner of Afghanistan, continued to report the highest levels of violence among all Afghan regional commands. For a complete account of the security situation in Afghanistan, see: U.S. Department of Defense, *Report on Progress Toward Security and Stability in Afghanistan,* 21-23.

[197] Barno, "Fighting "The Other War,"" 35.

[198] Center for Army Lessons Learned, *OEF Initial Impressions Report* (Fort

soldiers. Rocky terrain, drastic changes in elevation, and narrow footpaths constantly challenged

the fitness and coordination of ground troops as they patrolled the mountains and valleys of

Afghanistan.

Periodically, USF also conducted multi-day cordon and search operations. During these

missions units employed tactics similar to those developed during the decisive combat operation

phase of OEF, namely a contingent of dismounted ground troops supported extensively by

vehicle and aerial platforms before, during, and after the operation.[199] The most significant assets

incorporated during these events were U.S. Air Force CAS, AH-64 Apache CCA, and long-range

artillery fires. In *Vanguard of Valor*, the U.S. Army's study of small unit actions in Afghanistan,

Lieutenant Colonel John Mountcastle explains the importance of these platforms, stating

> The extreme terrain…in the Korengal, Waygal, and Chawkay valleys…usually prevented
> the basic tactical principles of identifying, closing with or even pursuing the enemy.

Leavenworth, KS: Center for Army Lessons Learned, December 2003), 18; Wright, *A Different Kind of War*, 251; K. Keefe, "Complacency Can Kill: Triple IED Ambush, Afghanistan 07/31/2003," in *Long Hard Road: NCO Experiences in Afghanistan and Iraq*, ed. L. R. Arms (Fort Bliss, TX: U.S. Army Sergeants Major Academy, 2007), 35; F. Gentry, "First Sergeant Role vs. Responsibility: 2nd Battalion, 27th Infantry, 25th ID, Afghanistan 03/04-03/05," in *Long Hard Road: NCO Experiences in Afghanistan and Iraq*, ed. L. R. Arms (Fort Bliss, TX: U.S. Army Sergeants Major Academy, 2007), 46; Scott J. Gaitley, "Ambushing the Taliban: A US Platoon in the Korengal Valley," in *Vanguard of Valor: Small Unit Actions in Afghanistan*, ed. Donald P. Wright (Fort Leavenworth, KS: Combat Studies Institute Press, 2011), 27-44; Matt M. Matthews, "Disrupt and Destroy: Platoon Patrol in Zhari District, September 2010," in *Vanguard of Valor: Small Unit Actions in Afghanistan*, ed. Donald P. Wright (Fort Leavenworth, KS: Combat Studies Institute Press, 2011), 131-152.

[199] Wright, *A Different Kind of War*, 252-253, 287; John C. Mountcastle, "Firefight above Gowardesh," in *Vanguard of Valor: Small Unit Actions in Afghanistan*, ed. Donald P. Wright (Fort Leavenworth, KS: Combat Studies Institute Press, 2011), 1-22; John J. McGrath, "Operation STRONG EAGLE: Combat Action in the Ghakhi Valley," in *Vanguard of Valor: Small Unit Actions in Afghanistan*, ed. Donald P. Wright (Fort Leavenworth, KS: Combat Studies Institute Press, 2011), 91-124; Kevin M. Hymel, "Trapping the Taliban at OP Dusty: A Scout Platoon in Zhari District," in *Vanguard of Valor: Small Unit Actions in Afghanistan*, ed. Donald P. Wright (Fort Leavenworth, KS: Combat Studies Institute Press, 2011), 157-173; Ryan D. Wadle, "Objective Lexington: Cougar Company under Fire in the Ganjgal Valley," in *Vanguard of Valor: Small Unit Actions in Afghanistan*, ed. Donald P. Wright (Fort Leavenworth, KS: Combat Studies Institute Press, 2011), 179-198.

Often, the exact location of the enemy was impossible to ascertain from the ground. As such, [soldiers] came to rely heavily on friendly aviation assets and aerial surveillance platforms. If they did not arrive already prepared to coordinate fire support missions, the [s]oldiers operating in northeastern Afghanistan would have to become adept at directing artillery and close air support. This skill was critical even for [s]oldiers at the squad level.[200]

As Mountcastle makes clear, throughout Afghanistan soldiers depended on technology to shift the balance of attack in their favor. On more than one occasion, CAS and CCA proved to be the critical factor which allowed an endangered unit to snatch victory from defeat.[201]

Beyond the dangers posed by the harsh Afghan terrain, AQ and Taliban remnants frequently attacked USF with a mixture of improvised explosive devices (IED), rocket-propelled grenades (RPG), mortars, and small arms fire. Enemy units often harassed USF patrols only briefly before retreating along hidden paths deep into the mountains. Periodically, however, these attacks evolved into coordinated, well-planned assaults on USF formations and facilities. Many attacks appeared intentionally designed to exploit the observable weaknesses in USF operations, such as deliberate ambushes emplaced on frequently used supply routes or the massing of forces to overrun lightly manned firebases.[202] For USF, the variety and intensity of these attacks irrevocably blurred the lines between combat operations and combat support operations; over time it became clear that any soldier, at any time, could become engaged in direct ground combat.[203] Doctrinally, the U.S. Army had anticipated this devolution in battlefield linearity.[204]

---

[200] John C. Mountcastle, "Firefight above Gowardesh," in *Vanguard of Valor*, 21-22.

[201] Matt M. Matthews, "Disrupt and Destroy: Platoon Patrol in Zhari District, September 2010," in *Vanguard of Valor*, 131-152; John C. Mountcastle, "Firefight above Gowardesh," in *Vanguard of Valor*, 1-22; Kevin M. Hymel, "Trapping the Taliban at OP Dusty: A Scout Platoon in Zhari District," in *Vanguard of Valor*, 157-173.

[202] Jerry Meyerle and Carter Malkasian, *Insurgent Tactics in Southern Afghanistan, 2005-2008* (Washington, D.C.: CNA Strategic Studies, August 2009).

[203] DACOWITS, *2009 Report*, 9-10.

However, it was former U.S. Army Chief of Staff General Peter Schoomaker who gave voice to

its reality in a 2003 speech before members of the Association of the United States Army.

Speaking to hundreds of the U.S. Army's staunchest public advocates, Schoomaker stated

> No longer is a Soldier's value measured by how close he or she is to the front line – there
> are no front lines on today's battlefield. Every Soldier is a warrior. Every Soldier has to
> embody not only the Army Values every day but take to heart the Soldier's Creed.[205]

In line with that creed, soldiers across Afghanistan "[stood] ready to deploy, engage, and destroy

the enemies of the United States of America in close combat."[206]

More than any previous campaign, OEF demonstrates the cognitive dissonance between

the Presidential Commission's understanding of war and the realities faced by soldiers on the

modern battlefield. Clearly, many of the challenges experienced by soldiers during a decade of

war in Afghanistan correspond with the assumptions made by the Presidential Commission.

Strength and stamina continue to play a part in direct ground combat. However, the evolution of

the non-linear battlefield now demands that all soldiers demonstrate the fitness to survive and

prevail in these conditions. In the words of COL Kevin Shwedo, U.S. Army Accessions

Command operations officer at the time of Schoomaker's statement and the officer responsible

---

[204] Touted as the "[U.S.] Army's keystone operations manual," the June 2001 version of
FM 3-0, *Operations*, formed the foundation of U.S. Army doctrine prior to the commencement of
OEF. The FM discussed the necessity of U.S. Army forces to conduct "full spectrum operations"
throughout the "range of military conflict," as well as provided guidance on the organization of
operations in a "non-linear battlefield." While it is unlikely that this version of FM 3-0 spurred
significant change in the limited time available after its publication and before OEF, the number
of enemy behaviors and doctrinal responses it presaged prompted units to swiftly incorporate and
adapt its concepts. For source of quotations and further information, see U.S. Department of the
Army, FM 3-0, *Operations* (Washington, D.C.: Headquarters, U.S. Department of the Army, June
2001).

[205] Reginald P. Rogers, "New Values Cards, Warrior Ethos 'dogtags' Available to Army
Units," *TRADOC News Service,* http://www-
tradoc.army.mil/pao/tnsarchives/September04/092304.htm (accessed March 27, 2013).

[206] U.S. Army, "Soldier's Creed," U.S. Army, www.army.mil/values/soldiers.html
(accessed March 27, 2013).

for the initial integration of the Warrior Ethos and Soldier's Creed, "Every Soldier has to be able to be an expert with his weapon. Every Soldier has to be physically fit. Every Soldier needs to know the warrior tasks and drills."[207] Given these conditions, the tactical and operational successes of OEF clearly indicate two things: first, the U.S. Army possesses the equipment and tactics to mitigate the extreme demands of direct ground combat; and second, U.S. Army soldiers—regardless of gender or MOS—are capable of leveraging those capabilities to outperform their enemies in direct ground combat. Based on this evidence, the operational risk posed to the U.S. Army by the revocation of the combat exclusion policy is low.

CONCLUSION

In the opening lines of *On War*, noted military theorist Carl von Clausewitz asks, "What is War?"[208] To answer his own question, Clausewitz offers to "proceed from the simple to the complex" and then begins by stating, "War is nothing but a duel on a larger scale."[209] Unfortunately, as this powerful, illustrative maxim is found on the first page of his multi-volume work, many readers default to this understanding of war and fail to grasp the nuance and complexity of the remainder of the book. These readers are not wrong; their understanding is simply incomplete. Much the same can be said for those who fail to account for both environment and performance when examining the operational risk associated with the revocation of the combat exclusion policy. In an effort to remedy this shortcoming, the following table provides a cross-tabular analysis of the assumptions made by the Presidential Commission regarding the

---

[207] Reginald P. Rogers, "New Values Cards, Warrior Ethos 'dogtags' Available to Army Units," *TRADOC News Service,* http://www-tradoc.army.mil/pao/tnsarchives/September04/092304.htm (accessed March 27, 2013).

[208] Carl von Clausewitz, *On War*, trans. and ed. Michael Howard and Peter Paret (Princeton, N.J.: Princeton University Press, 1984), 75.

[209] Carl von Clausewitz, *On War*, 75.

conditions and requirements of combat and the realities of war as presented in the above case studies.

Table 2. Cross-Tabular Analysis of Presidential Commission Assumptions and Case Study Evidence

	URGENT FURY	DESERT STORM DESERT SHIELD	ALLIED FORCE JOINT GUARDIAN	OEF
Frequency and Type of Mission				
Hand-to-Hand Combat	N	N	N	Y
Digging	N	Y	N	Y
Equipment Issued and Used				
Carrying Heavy Loads	Y	Y	Y	Y
Lifting Heavy Items	Y	Y	Y	Y
Austere Living Conditions				
	Y	Y	Y	Y
High Rate of Casualties				
	N	N	N	N
Treatment and Behavior of POW				
High Rate of Capture	N	N	N	N
Gendered Treatment of POW	N	Y	N	N

Source: Created by author.

From the table, it is clear that a number of the environmental concerns listed by the Presidential Commission continue to exist on the modern battlefield. For example, in all cases examined, soldiers routinely lifted and carried heavy equipment loads, as well as lived and worked in austere conditions. However, support for the Presidential Commission's assumptions in performance-oriented categories, such as casualty rates and the incidence of hand-to-hand fighting, is negligible. For instance, the total number of soldiers KIA during a hostile event in the

33.2 combat years covered by this study is 121 times less than the number of soldiers KIA during a hostile event in the 35.3 combat years from 1776-1981.[210] Viewed separately, neither the environmental data nor the performance data is wrong, just dangerously incomplete. When viewed together, however, they provide a much more nuanced understanding of the experiences of U.S. Army soldiers during this time period.

Put simply, while the conditions of combat did not change between 1982 and 2012, the way in which the U.S. Army fought did. Over the past thirty years the U.S. Army developed a number of advanced technologies designed to improve soldier survivability and lethality. Simultaneously, it evolved a warfighting doctrine that integrated the capabilities of this equipment to the fullest extent possible. Most recently, it expanded the audience for this doctrine and technology well beyond the traditional direct ground combat soldier. Afghanistan presented the ultimate test for these efforts, as the non-linear battlefield placed the majority of soldiers—regardless of MOS, gender, or physical ability—in direct ground combat situations.[211] Where the Presidential Commission predicted failure; the U.S. Army instead delivered overwhelming tactical and operational success. This result is clear and compelling. The U.S. Army possesses the willingness and ability to mitigate the hazards and demands posed by the modern battlefield. Furthermore, U.S. Army soldiers are trained and ready to prevail in direct ground combat. As a result, the revocation of the U.S. Army's combat exclusion policy poses a low operational risk to the force.

---

[210] See Appendix C, Casualty Rate Comparison, for full breakdown of casualty and POW rates experienced by the U.S. Army.

[211] DACOWITS, *2009 Report*, 9.

APPENDIX A – EXCERPT FROM THE PRESIDENTIAL COMMISSION ON THE ASSIGNMENT OF WOMEN IN THE ARMED FORCES' REPORT TO THE PRESIDENT, NOVEMBER 15, 1992

ISSUE K: GROUND COMBAT

Should the existing service policies restricting the assignment of servicewomen with respect to ground combat MOS/specialties be retained, modified, rescinded, or codified?

Recommendation: The sense of the Commission is that women should be excluded from direct land combat units and positions. Further, the Commission recommends that the existing service policies concerning direct land combat exclusions be codified. Service Secretaries shall recommend to the Congress which units and positions should fall under the land combat exclusion.

The issue of whether to retain, modify, rescind, or codify the policies restricting the assignment of women in ground combat specialties was statutorily required to be considered by the Commission. In addressing the issue, the Commission found the effectiveness of ground units to be the most significant criterion.

American military women are prohibited by Service policies that preclude them from serving in direct ground combat positions. Current policy excluding women from ground combat is based, in part, on Congressional intent to preclude women from serving in combat aircraft or on combatant ships. The specialties that fall under the exclusion may be grouped into four major areas: infantry, armor, artillery, and combat engineers, all of which require a soldier to be prepared to fight in direct, close-quarters combat.

Through testimony and trips, the Commission heard and observed that the daily life of the ground soldier in combat circumstances is one of constant physical exertion, often in extreme climactic conditions with the barest of amenities and the inherent risks of injury, capture and death. The Commission learned that despite technological advances, ground combat has not become less hazardous and physically demanding.

The evidence before the Commission clearly shows distinct physiological differences between men and women. Most women are shorter in stature, have less muscle mass and weigh less than men. These physiological differences place women at a distinct disadvantage when performing tasks requiring a high level of muscular strength and aerobic capacity, such as hand-to-hand fighting, digging, carrying heavy loads, lifting and other tasks central to ground combat.

The Commission also heard from women of tremendous physical ability who expressed a desire to serve in the ground combat arms. There is little doubt that some women could meet the physical standards for ground combat, but the evidence shows that few women possess the necessary physical qualifications. Further, a 1992 survey of 900 Army servicewomen shows that only 12 percent of enlisted women and ten percent of the female noncommissioned officers surveyed said they would consider serving in combat arms.

The Commission considered the effects that women could have on the cohesion of ground combat units. Cohesion is defined as the relationship that develops in a unit or group where: (1) members share common values and experiences; (2) individuals in the group conform to group norms and behavior in order to ensure group survival and goals; (3) members lose their personal identity in favor of a group identity; (4) members focus on group activities and goals; (5) members become totally dependent on each other for the completion of their mission or survival; and (6) members must meet all standards of performance and behavior in order not to threaten group survival. The evidence clearly shows that unit cohesion can be negatively affected by the introduction of any element that detracts from the need for such key ingredients as mutual confidence, commonality of experience, and equitable treatment. There are no authoritative military studies of mixed-gender ground combat cohesion, since available cohesion research has been conducted among male-only ground combat units.

One research study reviewed by the Commission indicates that the following are areas where cohesion problems might develop:

1.   Ability of women to carry the physical burdens required of each combat unit member. This entails an ability to meet physical standards of endurance and stamina.
2.   Forced intimacy and lack of privacy on the battlefield (e.g. washing, bathing, using latrine facilities, etc.).
3.   Traditional Western values where men feel a responsibility to protect women.
4.   Dysfunctional relationships (e.g. sexual misconduct).
5.   Pregnancy.

Of these, the prospect of sexual relationships in land units in direct combat with the enemy was considered to be dysfunctional and would encumber small unit ground combat leaders, noncommissioned officers, lieutenants and captains, in carrying out their military missions.

Ground combat incurs a high risk of capture by the enemy. The Commission's review of our nation's recent wars with respect to POWs suggests that potential enemies may not accord respect for the Geneva Convention and customary rules related to protection of prisoners. During our nation's major wars in this century, except Vietnam, the number of POWs has been greatest from the ground forces, the next largest number from downed aircraft and the least number from Navy ships. The Commission heard testimony from DoD representatives and POWs who indicated that the mistreatment of women taken as POWs could have a negative impact on male captives.

The Commission's enabling statute required examination of public attitudes toward the assignment of women in the military. Several surveys were conducted to determine what the American public and military attitudes were toward women in ground combat. The results of these surveys indicate that members of the military are strongly against women serving in all branches of ground combat, while the public has mixed views on service in different ground combat specialties. The Roper survey of the American public showed that 57 percent of the American public polled said that women should not be assigned to the infantry, and 52 percent were against women in Marine infantry. However, 58 percent of the public surveyed were in favor of assigning women to both artillery and armor positions.

The Roper military poll reported that 74 percent of the military members surveyed did not think women should serve in the infantry, 72 percent rejected the idea of women in Marine infantry, 59 percent opposed women in tank crews, and 54 percent did not want women to serve in the artillery. When the same question was asked of military personnel who had actually served in the ground combat arms, the numbers increased to 83 percent against women in the infantry, 83 percent against women serving in Marine infantry, 71 percent against women in armor, and 64 percent against women in artillery.

Several countries have placed women in ground combat units with little success. Historically, those nations that have permitted women in close combat situations (the Soviet Union, Germany, and Israel) have done so only because of grave threats to their national survival. After the crisis passed, each nation adopted policies which excluded the employment of women in combat. In more current times, the Commission learned that countries that have tested integrating women in ground combat units have found those tests unsuccessful.

The Commission also considered the effect on registration and conscription if women were allowed in ground combat units. In 1981, the Supreme Court upheld the male-only registration provision of the Military Selective Service Act, 50 U.S.C. App. 453, against a due process equal protection challenge from men who claimed that it was discriminatory because it required men, but not women, to register for the draft. The Court's opinion rested on the following argument: the purpose behind the registration requirement is to create a pool of individuals to be called up in the event of a draft; a draft is used to obtain combat troops; women are prevented, through law and policy, from serving in combat positions in any of the four Services; therefore, men and women are dissimilarly situated in regard to the registration requirement and it is permissible to treat them differently.

The Commission reviewed the assignment of draftees in our most recent conflicts, and according to statistics provided by DoD, 98 percent of draftees went to the Army during Vietnam, 95 percent during Korea and 83 percent during World War II. Because a draft is used to obtain combat troops and historically most draftees go into the Army, it can be deduced that the draft is used primarily to obtain a pool of ground combat troops. The Commission considered the possibility that lifting the ground combat exclusion pertaining to women may undermine the justification used by the Supreme Court to uphold the constitutionality of the all-male draft, because women would be eligible to serve in the positions which are filed through conscription.

The case against women in ground combat is compelling and conclusive. The physiological differences between men and women are most stark when compared to ground combat tasks. This is underscored by the evidence that there are few women, especially enlisted women, interested in serving in ground combat specialties. The overriding importance of small unit cohesion to ground military success, and the unknown but probably negative effect that the presence of women would have in those units were of critical concern to most Commissioners. Several polls revealed in most convincing terms that the public and military, especially the military people most familiar with its rigors, were fundamentally opposed to women in ground combat. The weight of international experience with women in ground combat units provides no conclusive evidence supporting the assignment of women in ground combat units. Finally, the legal implications of lifting the ground combat exclusion policy for the possible registration and conscription of women for ground combat were considered. The current ground combat exclusion policies, which are derived from Congressional intent to restrict the assignment of women in other Services, would be vulnerable if the remaining statute was repealed. The Commission therefore recommends that the ground exclusion policies be enacted into law for consistency and as sound public policy.

Commission Vote
Yes: *10*
No: *0*
Abstention: *2*[212]

---

[212] Presidential Commission, *Report to the President*, 24-27.

STANDARD U.S. ARMY FIGHTING LOAD, 1982-2012			
EQUIPMENT	**WEIGHT**	**EQUIPMENT**	**WEIGHT**
Advanced Combat Helmet	3.25	Meal, Ready to Eat	1.5
Belt, Standard Issue, Black	0.0625	Multi-Tool	0.5
Boots, Combat Black (pair)	4.0625	MOLLE 5.56mm ammunition pouch (2 total)	0.1875 (0.375 total)
Canteen, 1 Quart, with water (2 total)	2.5 ea. (5 total)	MOLLE canteen pouch (2 total)	0.375 (0.75 total)
Cup, Canteen	0.5	Rifle, M4	4.24
Desert Camouflage Patrol Cap	0.1875	Sling, Weapons, 3 Point Harness	0.375
Desert Camouflage Uniform Bottom	1.5625	Socks, Wool (pair)	0.1875
Desert Camouflage Uniform Top	1.5	Standard Field Dressing, with pouch	0.25
Drawers, Cotton	0.1875	Undershirt, Brown	0.375
Identification Tags	0.3125	Wrist watch	0.1875
Interceptor Body Armor, with 2 Small Arms Protective Inserts (SAPI) and no neck or crotch guard	17.5	Magazine, M16/M4 with 30-rounds (7 total)	1.375 (9.625 total)
			Total Weight: 52.49
STANDARD U.S. ARMY APPROACH MARCH LOAD, 1982-2012			
EQUIPMENT	**WEIGHT**	**EQUIPMENT**	**WEIGHT**
ALICE Rucksack	6	Flashlight	0.25
Desert Camouflage Uniform Bottom	1.5625	Night Vision Goggle, PVS-7D	1.25
Desert Camouflage Uniform Top	1.5	Poncho Liner	1.875
Drawers, Cotton (2 total)	0.1875 (0.375 total)	Socks, Wool (pair) (3 total)	0.1875 (0.5625 total)
Entrenching Tool with Carrier	3	Toiletries	2.5
Foot Powder	0.1875	Weapons Cleaning Kit, M16	0.3125
Gloves, Intermediate Cold Weather (Flyers)	0.375	Sun, Sand, and Dust type Goggles, ESS Model	0.875
Meal, Ready to Eat (3 total)	1.5 (4.5 total)	Undershirt, Brown (3 total)	0.375 (1.125 total)
			Total Weight: 26.25
Combined Total Weight, U.S. Army Soldier Combat Load, Adjusted*: 85			
STANDARD U.S. ARMY CHEMICAL PROTECTIVE LOAD, 1982-2012			
EQUIPMENT	**WEIGHT**	**EQUIPMENT**	**WEIGHT**
JSLIST Chemical and Biological Suit	5.5	Mask, Protective M45 with Carrier	3.0625
			Total Weight: 8.56
Combined Total Weight, U.S. Army Soldier Combat and Chemical Protective Load, Adjusted: 95**			

STANDARD U.S. ARMY SUSTAINMENT LOAD, 1982-2012			
EQUIPMENT	WEIGHT	EQUIPMENT	WEIGHT
Bag, Duffle (4 total)	2.0038 (8.0152 total)	Gortex, Light Weather Top	2.5625
Bag, Laundry	0.75	IPFU Jacket	1.1688
Bag, Waterproof (2 total)	0.1875 (0.375 total)	IPFU Pants	1.0625
Bib Overalls, CW Fleece Black	1.25	IPFU Shirt, Short Sleeve (2 total)	0.40625 (0.8125 total)
Boots, Combat Black	4.0625	IPFU Shirt, Long Sleeve	0.5875
Cap, Synthetic Micro-Fleece	0.125	IPFU Trunks (2 total)	0.29375 (0.5875 total)
ECWCS Polypropylene Drawers (3 total)	0.5625 (1.6875 total)	Knee Pads (pair)	0.625
ECWCS Polypropylene Undershirt (3 total)	0.6875 (2.0625 total)	Mat, Sleeping, Self-Inflating	1.3125
ECWCS Silk Weight Drawers (2 total)	0.31 (0.62 total)	Modular Sleep Bag System	11.06
ECWCS Silk Weight Undershirt (2 total)	0.44 (0.88 total)	Neck Gaiter	0.0625
Elbow Pads (pair)	0.9375	On-The-Move Hydration System	0.75
Field Jacket	3.0875	Parka, Wet Weather	1.4313
Field Jacket Liner	0.7563	Poncho, Wet Weather	1.3125
Gortex, Cold Weather Bottom	3.4375	Shirt, CW Fleece Black	2.31
Gortex, Cold Weather Top	4.0625	Socks, Wool (pair) (2 total)	0.1875 (0.375 total)
Gortex, Light Weather Bottom	2.5625	Trousers, Wet Weather	1.3125
			Total Weight: 62
NOTES			
*6.26 lbs. have been added to the original combined total weight of 78.74 in an effort to account for variances in materials used during this time period and individual deviations from the packing list, as well as for ease of calculation.			
**7.7 lbs. have been added to the original combined total weight of 87.3 lbs. in an effort to account for variances in materials used during this time period and individual deviations from the packing list, as well as for ease of calculation.			
***All weights in pounds			

Source: Task Force Devil CAAT, The Modern Warrior's Combat Load: Dismounted Operations in Afghanistan, April-May 2003, (Fort Leavenworth: U.S. Army CALL, 2003), 107-111; United States Department of the Army, Personnel Policy Guidance for Overseas Contingency Operations, (Washington D.C.: U.S. Department of the Army, 2009), Chapter 10. Calculations completed by author.

Conflict	Length of Conflict (Years)	Total Hostile KIA	Annual Average Hostile KIA	Total Non-Hostile KIA	Annual Average Non-Hostile KIA	Total WIA	Annual Average WIA	Total POW	Annual Average POW
U.S. ARMY CASUALTY DATA AND RATES, 1776-1981									
Revolutionary War	8.0	4,044.0	505.5	-	-	6,004.0	750.5	-	-
War of 1812	3.0	1,950.0	650.0	-	-	4,000.0	133.3	-	-
Mexican War	2.0	1,721.0	860.5	11,550.0	5,775.0	4,102.0	2,051.0	-	-
*Civil War	4.0	138,154.0	34,538.5	221,374.0	55,343.5	280,040.0	70,010.0	-	-
Spanish-American War	0.3	369.0	369.0	2,061.0	2,061.0	1,594.0	1,594.0	-	-
WWI	1.0	50,510.0	50,510.0	55,868.0	55,868.0	193,663.0	193,663.0	-	-
**WWII	5.0	234,874.0	46,974.8	83,400.0	16,680.0	565,861.0	113,172.2	124,079.0	24,815.8
Korean War	3.0	27,731.0	9,243.7	2,125.0	708.3	77,596.0	25,865.3	6,656.0	2,218.6
Vietnam	9.0	30,963.0	3,440.3	7,261.0	806.8	201,525.0	22,391.5	167.0	18.5
	Total Conflict Length (Years)	Total Conflict Hostile KIA	Total Conflict Annual Average Hostile KIA	Total Conflict Non-Hostile KIA	Total Conflict Annual Average Non-Hostile KIA	Total Conflict WIA	Total Conflict Annual Average WIA	Total Conflict POW	Total Conflict Annual Average POW
All Conflicts	35.3 (17 POW)	490,316.0	13,890.0	383,639.0	10,868.0	1,334,385.0	37,801.2	130,902.0	7,700.1
U.S. ARMY CASUALTY DATA AND RATES, 1982-2012									
Conflict	Length of Conflict (Years)	Total Hostile KIA	Annual Average Hostile KIA	Total Non-Hostile KIA	Annual Average Non-Hostile KIA	Total WIA	Annual Average WIA	Total POW	Annual Average POW
***URGENT FURY	0.1	11.0	11.0	1.0	1.0	108.0	108.0	0.0	0.0
****JUST CAUSE	0.1	18.0	18.0	0.0	0.0	322.0	322.0	0.0	0.0
*****DESERT SHIELD, DESERT STORM	1.0	224.0	224.0	98.0	98.0	354.0	354.0	21.0	21.0
******ALLIED FORCE, JOINT GUARDIAN	13.0	0.0	0.0	0.0	0.0	25.0	1.9	0.0	0.0
OEF	9.0	2,574.0	286.0	819.0	91.0	22,546.0	2,505.1	0.0	0.0
OIF	10.0	1,223.0	122.3	297.0	29.7	12,851.0	1,285.1	6.0	0.6
	Total Conflict Length (Years)	Total Conflict Hostile KIA	Total Conflict Annual Average Hostile KIA	Total Conflict Non-Hostile KIA	Total Conflict Annual Average Non-Hostile KIA	Total Conflict WIA	Total Conflict Annual Average WIA	Total Conflict POW	Total Conflict Annual Average POW
All Conflicts	33.2	4,050.0	122.0	1,215.0	36.6	36,206.0	1,091.0	27.0	0.8

(-) Indicates lack of available data.

*Totals Include Union Forces Only.

**Totals Include U.S. Army Air Corps.

***WIA Data from: Raines, Jr., *The Rucksack War*, 532.

****WIA totals include all U.S. military; WIA Data from: Stewart, *Operation JUST CAUSE*, 44.

*****POW Totals Include All Branches of Service. POW Data from: Klein, et al., *American Prisoners of War (POWs) and Missing in Action (MIAs)*, 8.

******KIA, WIA, and POW data for this conflict not available from the Defense Manpower Data Center. Information provided from: Phillips, *Operation JOINT GUARDIAN*, 14, 39, 49.

Source: Defense Manpower Data Center, unless otherwise noted. Calculations completed by author.

BIBLIOGRAPHY

3rd Brigade, 101st Airborne Division (Air Assault). *Operation DESERT SHIELD / Operation DESERT STORM Yearbook*. Paducha, KY: Turner Publishing Company, 1992.

10th Mountain Division. *Hypovolemic Shock Management: Combat Medic Advanced Skills Training*. Brief, n.d.

101st Airborne Division (Air Assault). "101st Airborne Division History." 101st Airborne Division Homepage. http://www.campbell.army.mil/units/101st/Pages/History.aspx (accessed March 14, 2013).

Antigua, Dominica, Grenada, Montserrat, St. Kitts/Nevis, Saint Lucia, and Saint Vincent and the Grenadines. "Treaty Establishing the Organization of Eastern Caribbean States." June 18, 1981. *United Nations Treaty Series: Treaties and International Agreements Registered or Filed and Recorded with the Secretariat of the United Nations* 1338, no. I-22435 (1981).

Bacon, Kenneth. "U.S. Department of Defense News Briefing, March 23, 1999." U.S. Department of Defense Office of the Assistant Secretary of Defense (Public Affairs). http://www.defense.gov/transcripts/transcript.aspx?transcriptid=632 (accessed March 17, 2013).

Barno, David W. "Fighting "The Other War:" Counterinsurgency Strategy in Afghanistan, 2003-2005." *Military Review* (September-October 2007): 32-44.

Beardsley, Steven. "Active-duty Troops to Deploy to Kosovo for First Time in a Decade." *Stripes.com*, March 13, 2013. http://www.stripes.com/news/active-duty-troops-to-deploy-to-kosovo-for-first-time-in-a-decade-1.211663 (accessed March 19, 2013).

Bennett, Christopher. *Yugoslavia's Bloody Collapse: Causes, Course, and Consequences*. Washington Square, NY: New York University Press, 1995.

Berg, Steven L. and Paul S. Shoup. *The War in Bosnia-Herzegovina: Ethnic Conflict and International Intervention*. Armonk, NY: M.E. Sharp, 1999.

Berry, D. "Establishing a Special Forces Firebase: ODA 381, 3rd Bn, 3rd SFG (Airborne)." In *Long Hard Road: NCO Experiences in Afghanistan and Iraq*, edited by L. R. Arms, 59-52. Fort Bliss, TX: U.S. Army Sergeants Major Academy, 2007.

Boffen, Jerry. "KFOR 12 Commander Holds Final Meeting with Kosovo Media." *NG.mil*, July 9, 2010. http://www.ng.mil/news/archives/2010/07/070910-KFOR.aspx (accessed March 19, 2013).

Bohannon, Richard M. "Dragon's Roar: 1-37 Armor in the Battle of 73 Easting." *Armor* 101, no. 3 (May-June 1992): 11-17.

Bolt, William J. "Command Report, 101st Airborne Division (Air Assault) for operations Desert Shield and Desert Storm, 2 August 1990 through 1 May 1991," Memorandum for Commander, XVIII Airborne Corps. Fort Campbell, KY, July 1, 1991.

Bourque, Stephen A. *Jayhawk! The VII Corps in the Persian Gulf War.* Washington D.C.: U.S. Department of the Army, 2002.

Bourque, Stephen A. and John W. Burdan III. *The Road to Safwan: The 1ˢᵗ Squadron, 4ᵗʰ Cavalry in the 1991 Persian Gulf War.* Denton, TX: University of North Texas Press, 2007.

Bowen, Beverly. "Grenadians are Shocked, Bewildered." *The Globe and Mail,* October 21, 1983.

Brown, Kingsley. *Co-Ed Combat: The New Evidence That Women Shouldn't Fight the Nation's Wars.* New York: Penguin, 2007.

Bush, George H. W. "Address on Iraq's Invasion of Kuwait." *Public Papers of the Presidents of the United States* (August 8, 1990). http://millercenter.org/president/speeches/detail/5529 (accessed March 11, 2013).

———, George H. W. National Security Directive 45. "U.S. Policy in Response to the Iraqi Invasion of Kuwait." August 20, 1990.

Bush, George W. "Address to a Joint Session of Congress and the American People." *Public Papers of the Presidents of the United States* (September 20, 2001). http://georgewbush-whitehouse.archives.gov/news/releases/2001/09/20010920-8.html (accessed March 19, 2013).

———, George W. "Address to the Nation on the Terrorist Attacks." *Public Papers of the Presidents of the United States* (September 11, 2001). http://www.presidency.ucsb.edu/ws/index.php?pid=58057 (accessed March 19, 2013).

———, George W. "Letter to Congressional Leaders Reporting on the Deployment of United States Military Personnel as Part of the Kosovo International Security Force." *Weekly Compilation of Presidential Documents* (June 12, 1999).

———, George W. "Letter to Congressional Leaders Reporting on the Deployment of United States Military Personnel as Part of the Kosovo International Security Force." *Weekly Compilation of Presidential Documents* (June 16, 2000).

———, George W. "Letter to Congressional Leaders Reporting on the Deployment of United States Military Personnel as Part of the Kosovo International Security Force." *Weekly Compilation of Presidential Documents* (May 18, 2001).

———, George W. "Letter to Congressional Leaders Reporting on the Deployment of United States Military Personnel as Part of the Kosovo International Security Force." *Weekly Compilation of Presidential Documents* (May 14, 2003).

———, George W. "Letter to Congressional Leaders Reporting on Deployment of United States Combat-Equipped Armed Forces Around the World." *Weekly Compilation of Presidential Documents* (May 20, 2005).

————, George W. "Letter to Congressional Leaders Reporting on Deployments of United States Combat-Equipped Armed Forces Around the World." *Weekly Compilation of Presidential Documents* (June 15, 2006).

————, George W. "Letter to Congressional Leaders Reporting on Deployments of United States Combat-Equipped Armed Forces Around the World." *Weekly Compilation of Presidential Documents* (June 15, 2007).

————, George W. "Letter to Congressional Leaders Reporting on the Deployments of United States Combat-Equipped Armed Forces Around the World." *Weekly Compilation of Presidential Documents* (June 13, 2008).

Carlson, Anthony E. "Forging Alliances at Yargul Village: A Lieutenant's Struggle to Improve Security." In *Vanguard of Valor: Small Unit Actions in Afghanistan*, edited by Donald P. Wright, 73-87. Fort Leavenworth, KS: Combat Studies Institute Press, 2011.

Carter, Jimmy. *Public Papers of the Presidents of the United States.* http://www.presidency.ucsb.edu/ws/index.php?pid=33079 (accessed March 10, 2013).

Cheeseborough, Randall K. "Multiple Launch Rocket System (MLRS) Deep Fires." *Joint Center for Lessons Learned Bulletin* 2, no. 2 (June 2000): 19-29.

Cheney, Richard B. "Army Operations Update—Information Memorandum Number 1." Memorandum for Secretary of the Army and Chief of Staff of the Army. Washington D.C., August 8, 1990.

CJTF Mountain. *Afghanistan and Operation ANACONDA.* Brief, n.d.

Clark, Wesley K. *Waging Modern War.* New York, NY: PublicAffairs, 2001.

Clausewitz, Carl von. *On War.* Translated and edited by Michael Howard and Peter Paret. Princeton, N.J.: Princeton University Press, 1984.

Clinton, William J. "Statement on Kosovo." *Public Papers of the Presidents of the United States* (March 24, 1999). http://millercenter.org/president/speeches/detail/3932 (accessed March 17, 2013).

Cole, Ronald H. *Operation URGENT FURY: The Planning and Execution of Joint Operations in Grenada, 12 October -2 November 1983.* Washington, D.C.: Joint History Office, Office of the Chairman of the Joint Chiefs of Staff, 1997.

Countermine Counter Booby Trap Center. "Operation DESERT SHIELD and Operation DESERT STORM Lessons Learned." After Action Review, n.d.

Crawley, Vince. "Ghost Troop's Battle at the 73 Easting." *Armor* 100, no. 3 (May-June 1991): 7-12.

C-SPAN. "Iraqi Invasion of Kuwait." C-SPAN Video Library, http://www.c-spanvideo.org/program/13395-1 (accessed March 10, 2013).

Curthoys, Kathleen. "Readers Question Putting Women In Combat." *Army Times*, February 4, 2013.

Daalder, Ivo H. and Michael E. O'Hanlon. *Winning Ugly: NATO's War to Save Kosovo*. Washington, D.C.: Brookings Institution Press, 2000.

Davis, Daniel L. "The 2d ACR at the Battle of 73 Easting." *Field Artillery* (April 1992): 48-53.

Defense Manpower Data Center. "Active Duty Military Deaths by Year and Manner (1980-2010)." Defense Casualty Analysis System. https://www.dmdc.osd.mil/dcas/pages/report_by_year_manner.xhtml (accessed March 25, 2013).

———. "Principal Wars in Which the United States Participated – U.S. Military Personnel Serving and Casualties (1775-1991)." Defense Casualty Analysis System. https://www.dmdc.osd.mil/dcas/pages/report_principal_wars.xhtml (accessed March 18, 2012).

———. "U.S. Military Casualties – Persian Gulf War Casualty Summary Desert Shield." Defense Casualty Analysis System. https://www.dmdc.osd.mil/dcas/pages/report_gulf_shield.xhtml (accessed March 12, 2013).

———. "Worldwide U.S. Active Duty Military Deaths: Selected Military Operations (1980-1996)." Defense Casualty Analysis System. https://www.dmdc.osd.mil/dcas/pages/report_operations.xhtml (accessed November 28, 2012).

Dempsey, Martin E. "Women in the Service Implementation Plan," Memorandum for Secretary of Defense. Washington D.C., January 9, 2013.

Ebben, William P. and Randall L. Jensen. "Strength Training for Women: Debunking the Myths That Block Opportunity." *The Physician and Sportsmedicine* 26, no. 5 (May 1998): 2.

Flanagan, Jr., Edward M. *Lightning: The 101st in the Gulf War*. Washington: Brassey's (US), Inc., 1994.

Flemming, Lee A. "The Way Ahead: Lessons from Gnjilane, Kosovo." *Infantry* 91, no. 1 (Spring 2002): 28-31.

Forro, W. "Building a Forward Operating Base: 2nd Battalion, 5th Infantry Battalion." In *Long Hard Road: NCO Experiences in Afghanistan and Iraq*, edited by L. R. Arms, 66-69. Fort Bliss, TX: U.S. Army Sergeants Major Academy, 2007.

Franks, Tommy R. *American Soldier*. New York, NY: HarperCollins, 2004.

Frazier, Lindsey M. "Face of Defense: Mother, Son Prepare to Deploy to Kosovo Together." *Defense.gov*, May 15, 2008. http://www.defense.gov/News/NewsArticle.aspx?ID=49881 (accessed March 19, 2013).

Gaitley, Scott J. "Ambushing the Taliban: A US Platoon in the Korengal Valley." In *Vanguard of Valor: Small Unit Actions in Afghanistan*, edited by Donald P. Wright 27-47. Fort Leavenworth, KS: Combat Studies Institute Press, 2011.

Gates, Robert M. *Quadrennial Defense Review.* Washington, D.C.: U.S. Department of Defense, February 2010.

Gentry, F. "First Sergeant Role vs. Responsibility: 2nd Battalion, 27th Infantry, 25th ID, Afghanistan 03/04-03/05." In *Long Hard Road: NCO Experiences in Afghanistan and Iraq*, edited by L. R. Arms 45-47. Fort Bliss, TX: U.S. Army Sergeants Major Academy, 2007.

Gholston, L. "Air Medical Evacuation: 68th Medical Company Air Ambulance, Afghanistan 11/03-11/04." In *Long Hard Road: NCO Experiences in Afghanistan and Iraq*, edited by L. R. Arms, 38-41. Fort Bliss, TX: U.S. Army Sergeants Major Academy, 2007.

Greenhill, Jim. "National Guard's Critical Role in Kosovo." *NG.mil*, May 25, 2007. http://www.ng.mil/news/archives/2007/05/052507-kosovo.aspx (accessed March 19, 2013).

Gregor, William. "Why Can't Anything Be Done? Measuring Physical Readiness of Women for Military Occupations." Paper presented at the 2011 International Biennial Conference of the Inter-University Seminar on Armed Forces and Society, Chicago IL, October 21-23, 2011.

Gooden, Reginald R. "Experiences during Operations Desert Shield/Storm: Operations Desert Shield/Storm, Iraq, 08/12/90 thru 04/01/91, 91B1P, Infantry Platoon Combat Line Medic, A Company, 1/505th PIR, 82d ABN DIV." United States Army Sergeant Majors Academy Personal Experience Papers Collection. Combined Arms Research Library, Fort Leavenworth, KS.

Hagburg, Michael. "Kosovo Force to Transform into Deterrent Presence." *Defense.gov*, January 5, 2010. http://www.defense.gov/news/newsarticle.aspx?id=57362 (accessed March 19, 2013).

Hall, L. "Make a Way: 725th Main Support Battalion, Afghanistan, 03/04-02/05." In *Long Hard Road: NCO Experiences in Afghanistan and Iraq*, edited by L. R. Arms 42-45. Fort Bliss, TX: U.S. Army Sergeants Major Academy, 2007.

Harman, Everett, Peter Frykman, Christopher Palmer, Eric Lammi, Katy Reynolds, and Verne Backus. "Effects of a Specifically Designed Physical Conditioning Program on the Load Carriage and Lifting Performance of Female Soldiers." Technical report, U.S. Army Research of Environmental Medicine, November 1997.

Harper, Gilbert S. "Logistics in Grenada: Supporting No-Plan Wars." *Parameters* 20, (June 1990): 50-63.

Harrell, Margaret C. and Laura L. Miller. *New Opportunities for Military Women: Effects Upon Readiness, Cohesion, and Morale.* Santa Monica, CA: Rand, 1997.

Hillen, John. "2d Armored Cavalry: The Campaign to Liberate Kuwait." *Armor* 100, no. 4 (July-August 1991): 8-12.

Hope, Ian. "Unity of Command in Afghanistan: A Forsaken Principle of War." Carlisle paper, U.S., Army War College, November 2008.

Houlahan, Thomas. *Gulf War: The Complete History*. New London, NH: Schrenker Military Publishing, 1999.

Hymel, Kevin M. "Trapping the Taliban at OP Dusty: A Scout Platoon in Zhari District." In *Vanguard of Valor: Small Unit Actions in Afghanistan*, edited by Donald P. Wright 157-173. Fort Leavenworth, KS: Combat Studies Institute Press, 2011.

"International." *New York Times*, November 5, 1983.

"International." *New York Times*, November 6, 1983.

International Security Assistance Force. "History." International Security Assistance Force, http://www.isaf.nato.int/history.html (accessed March 24, 2013).

"Invasion in Grenada." *New York Times*, October 28, 1983.

Johnson, Ray B., Scott Campbell, Mark E. Moore, Frankie Marrero, and Sue Parnell-Smith. "The Light Infantry Division." Group paper, United States Army Sergeant Majors Academy, 2005.

Junger, Sebastian. *War*. New York, NY: 12, 2010.

Keefe, K. "Complacency Can Kill: Triple IED Ambush, Afghanistan 07/31/2003." In *Long Hard Road: NCO Experiences in Afghanistan and Iraq*, edited by L. R. Arms 35-37. Fort Bliss, TX: U.S. Army Sergeants Major Academy, 2007.

Kirk, Kathleen F. "Women in Combat?" Report presented to the Faculty of the School of Education in partial fulfillment of the Requirements for the course Education 795 A&B Seminar, San Diego State University, 1988.

Kirkpatrick, Charles E. *"Ruck It Up! The Post-Cold War Transformation of V Corps, 1990-2001.* Washington, D.C.: Department of the Army, 2006.

Kozaryn, Linda D. "Life as a U.S. Peacekeeper in Kosovo." *Defense.gov*, December 27, 1999. http://www.defense.gov/news/newsarticle.aspx?id=42907 (accessed March 19, 2013).

————, Linda D. "SHAPE Considers Troop Needs for Kosovo Force." *Defense.gov*, April 6, 2000. http://www.defense.gov/news/newsarticle.aspx?id=45087 (accessed March 19, 2013).

Krivda, Erik and Kamil Sztalkoper. "Conducting Vehicle Checkpoints in Kosovo." *Infantry* 92, no. 2 (Winter 2003): 16-18.

"The Liberation of Mazar-e Sharif: 5h SF Group Conducts UW in Afghanistan." *Special Warfare* 15, no. 2 (June 2002): 34-41.

Lednar, Wayne M. and Gregory A. Poland. "Recommendations Regarding the Tactical Combat Casualty Care Guidelines on Fluid Resuscitation 2010-07." Memorandum for George Peach Taylor, Jr. M.D., December 10, 2010.

Lukach, Terri. "Kosovo Mission Successful, Important, U.S. Forces Say." *Defense.gov*, August 15, 2005. http://www.defense.gov/news/newsarticle.aspx?id=16883 (accessed March 19, 2013).

McDonnell, Janet A. *After DESERT STORM: The U.S. Army and the Reconstruction of Kuwait.* Washington, D.C.: Department of the Army, 1999.

McGrath, John J. "Operation STRONG EAGLE: Combat Action in the Ghakhi Valley." In *Vanguard of Valor: Small Unit Actions in Afghanistan*, edited by Donald P. Wright 91-124. Fort Leavenworth, KS: Combat Studies Institute Press, 2011.

McGuire, P. "Task Force Rakkasan: 3-101st, Aviation Regiment 03/02-08/02." In *Long Hard Road: NCO Experiences in Afghanistan and Iraq*, edited by L. R. Arms, 18-20. Fort Bliss, TX: U.S. Army Sergeants Major Academy, 2007.

McHugh, John. "Army Directive 2012-16 (Changes to Army Policy for the Assignment of Female Soldiers)." Memorandum for Commanders, U.S. Army Major Commands. Washington, D.C. June 27, 2012.

MacCoun, Robert J. Elizabeth Kier and Aaron Belkin. "Does Social Cohesion Determine Motivation in Combat? An Old Question with an Old Answer." *Armored Forces and Society* 32, no. 4 (July 2006): 646-654.

Malcolm, Noel. *Kosovo: A Short History*. New York, NY: HarperPerennial, 1999.

Maggart, Lon E. "A Leap of Faith." *Armor* 101, no. 1 (January-February 1992): 24-32.

Matthews, Matt M. "Disrupt and Destroy: Platoon Patrol in Zhari District, September 2010," In *Vanguard of Valor: Small Unit Actions in Afghanistan*, edited by Donald P. Wright 131-152. Fort Leavenworth, KS: Combat Studies Institute Press, 2011.

Meyerle, Jerry and Carter Malkasian. *Insurgent Tactics in Southern Afghanistan, 2005-2008*. Washington, D.C.: CNA Strategic Studies, August 2009.

Meyerle, Jerry, Megan Katt, and Jim Gabrilis. "A US Army Battalion in Kunar and Nuristan, 2007-2008." In *Counterinsurgency on the Ground in Afghanistan: How Different Units Adapted to Local Conditions*, 51-61. Washington, D.C.: CNA Strategic Studies, 2010.

Meyerle, Jerry, Megan Katt, and Jim Gabrilis. "A US Army Battalion in Khost, 2004-2008." In *Counterinsurgency on the Ground in Afghanistan*, 63-69. Washington, D.C.: CNA Strategic Studies, 2010.

Meyerle, Jerry, Megan Katt, and Jim Gabrilis. "A US Army Battalion in Nangarhar Province, 2005-2009." In *Counterinsurgency on the Ground in Afghanistan,* 71-82. Washington, D.C.: CNA Strategic Studies, 2010.

Miles, Donna. "Kosovo Force Prepares for Political Status Resolution." *Defense.gov,* November 15, 2006. http://www.defense.gov/news/newsarticle.aspx?id=2125 (accessed March 19, 2013).

———, Donna. "U.S. Commander Condemns Attacks on Kosovo Force." *Defense.gov,* November 29, 2011. http://www.defense.gov/news/newsarticle.aspx?id=66279 (accessed March 19, 2013).

———, Donna. "Kosovo Force Rotation Prepares for Peacekeeping Mission." *Defense.gov,* August 31, 2012. http://www.defense.gov/News/NewsArticle.aspx?ID=117702 (accessed March 19, 2013).

Mitzel, Dennis R. "When Will We Listen?" Research report, Air War College, April 1997.

Morris, Roberta. "Grenadians Recount Horror of PM's Killing." *Toronto Star*, May 11, 1986.

Mountcastle, John C. "Firefight above Gowardesh." In *Vanguard of Valor: Small Unit Actions in Afghanistan*, edited by Donald P. Wright 1-22. Fort Leavenworth, KS: Combat Studies Institute Press, 2011.

Nardulli, Bruce R., Walter L. Perry, Bruce Pirnie, John Gordon IV, and John G. McGinn. *Disjointed War: Military Operations in Kosovo, 1999*. Santa Monica, CA: RAND, 2002.

Nation, R. Craig. *War in the Balkans: 1991-2002*. Washington D.C.: Strategic Studies Institute, 2003.

National Center for Ecological Analysis and Synthesis (NCEAS). "Commercial Activity (Shipping)." NCEAS. http://www.nceas.ucsb.edu/globalmarine/impacts (accessed November 26, 2012).

National Commission on Terrorist Attacks Upon the United States. *Testimony of U.S. Secretary of Defense Donald H. Rumsfeld,* March 23, 2004.

North Atlantic Treaty Organization. "Military Technical Agreement Between the International Security Force ("KFOR") and the Governments of the Federal Republic of Yugoslavia and the Republic of Serbia." http://www.nato.int/koSovo/docu/a990609a.htm (accessed March 18, 2013).

———. "KFOR Press Statements and News Conferences." http://www.nato.int/kosovo/jnt-grdn.htm (accessed March 18, 2013).

Norton, David. "Cecil's Ride: A Tank Platoon Leader In Desert Storm." *Armor* 113, no. 6 (November-December 1999): 30-35.

Obama, Barack. "Letter to Congressional Leaders on the Global Deployments of United States Combat-Equipped Armed Forces." *Weekly Compilation of Presidential Documents* (June 15, 2009).

————, Barack. "Letter to Congressional Leaders on the Global Deployments of United States Combat-Equipped Armed Forces." *Weekly Compilation of Presidential Documents* (June 15, 2010).

————, Barack. "Letter to Congressional Leaders on the Global Deployments of United States Combat-Equipped Armed Forces." *Weekly Compilation of Presidential Documents* (June 15, 2011).

————, Barack. "Letter to Congressional Leaders on the Deployment of United States Combat-Equipped Armed Forces." *Weekly Compilation of Presidential Documents* (June 15, 2012).

"Operation Anaconda Costs 8 U.S. Lives." *CNN World*, March 4, 2002. http://articles.cnn.com/2002-03-04/world/ret.afghan.fighting_1_shahi-kot-afghan-forces-qaeda-and-taliban?_s=PM:asiapcf (accessed March 23, 2013).

Operation Anaconda Combat Operations Brief. Brief, CJTF Mountain, February 26, 2002.

Pennsylvania Army National Guard. "KFOR 5A – Pennsylvania Army National Guard," YouTube.com, Windows Media Player video file. http://www.youtube.com/watch?v=2tTEuwjZQrw (accessed March 19, 2013).

Perera, David. "Camp Bondsteel: They Call it 'Little America.'" *Defense Standard* (Fall 2008). http://www.davidperera.com/Perera_DefStan_Camp%20Bondsteel.pdf (accessed March 18, 2013).

Peterson, C. "Baptism by Fire: 705th Ordnance Company, Afghanistan 10/02-06/03." In *Long Hard Road: NCO Experiences in Afghanistan and Iraq*, edited by L. R. Arms, 28-34. Fort Bliss, TX: U.S. Army Sergeants Major Academy, 2007.

Porter, Laurie M. and Rick V. Adside. "Women in Combat: Attitudes and Experiences of U.S. Military Officers and Enlisted Personnel." Master's thesis, Naval Postgraduate School, 2001.

Powell, Colin L. "Execute Order for Operation DESERT STORM." Washington D.C., January 15, 1991.

Phillips, R. Cody. *Operation JOINT GUARDIAN: The U.S. Army in Kosovo.* Washington, D.C.: Center of Military History, 2007.

————, R. Cody. *Operation JUST CAUSE: The Incursion into Panama.* Washington, D.C.: Center of Military History, 2004.

Puryear, A. A. and Gerald R. Haywood, II. "Ar Rumaylah Airfield Succumbs to Hasty Attack." *Armor* 100, no. 5 (September-October 1991): 16-20.

Raines, Jr., Edgar F. *The Rucksack War: U.S. Army Operational Logistics in Grenada, 1983.* Washington D.C.: Center of Military History, 2010.

Reagan, Ronald. *Public Papers of the Presidents of the United States: Ronald Reagan, 1983.* 2 vols. Washington, D.C.: United States Government Printing Office, 1984.

———, Ronald. National Security Decision Directive no. 105. "Eastern Caribbean Regional Security Policy." *Code of Federal Regulations*, title 3. http://www.fas.org/irp/offdocs/nsdd/nsdd-105.pdf (accessed November 26, 2012).

Reese, Timothy R., Kevin W. Farrell, and Matthew P. Moore. "An Armor Battalion in Kosovo." *Armor* 108, no. 6 (November-December 1999): 26-29.

Rogers, Reginald P. "New Values Cards, Warrior Ethos 'dogtags' Available to Army Units." *TRADOC News Service,* September 24, 2004. http://www-tradoc.army.mil/pao/tnsarchives/September04/092304.htm (accessed March 27, 2013).

Rose II, Peter W. "American Armor in Albania, A Soldier's Mosaic." *Armor* 108, no. 4 (July-August 1999): 8-9, 50-51.

———, Peter W. and Keith Flowers. "Task Force HAWK Command and Control." *Joint Center for Lessons Learned Bulletin* 2, no. 2 (June 2000): 1-9.

Rosen, Leora N., Kathryn H. Knudson, and Peggy Fancher. "Cohesion and the Culture of Hypermasculinity in U.S. Army Units." *Armed Forces and Society* 29, no. 3 (Spring 2003): 325-351.

Rumsfeld, Donald H. *Quadrennial Defense Review.* Washington, D.C.: U.S. Department of Defense, February 2006).

Scales, Jr., Robert H. *Certain Victory: The U.S. Army in the Gulf War.* Washington, D.C.: Center for Military History, 1994.

Schubert, Frank N. and Theresa L. Kraus, eds. *The Whirlwind War: The United States Army in Operations DESERT SHIELD and DESERT STORM.* Washington, D.C.: Center of Military History, 1995.

Schult, Marie. "Operation Valiant Strike." *Army* 53, no. 5 (May 2003): 59-60.

Scott, Michael. "A Taste of Life at Outpost SAPPER: Supporting Peace on a Volatile Border." *Armor* 111, no. 3 (May-June 2001): 11-12, 39.

Seixas, Suzanne. "A Soldier Without Fortune: Ex-P.O.W. Troy Dunlap returns to a hero's welcome, a new baby—and $18,000 of debt." CNN Money, May 1, 1991. http://money.cnn.com/magazines/moneymag/moneymag_archive/1991/05/01/86516/index.htm (accessed March 25, 2013).

Sellers, Russell. "Post Honors Outstanding Employee." U.S. Army. http://www.army.mil/article/67629/Post_honors_outstanding_employee/ (accessed March 23, 2013).

Silber, Laura and Allan Little. *Yugoslavia: Death of a Nation*. U.S.: TV Books, 1995.

Spector, Ronald. *U.S. Marines in Grenada, 1983*. Washington, D.C.: Headquarters, U.S. Marine Corps History and Museums Division, 1987.

Springer, Nathan. "Implementing a Population-Centric Counterinsurgency Strategy: Northeast Afghanistan, May 07-July 08." *Small Wars Journal* (2010).

Stewart, Richard W. *Operation ENDURING FREEDOM: The United States Army in Afghanistan, October 2001 – March 2002*. Washington, D.C.: Center of Military History, 2004.

———, Richard W. *Operation Urgent Fury: The Invasion of Grenada, October 1983*. Washington D.C.: Center of Military History, 2008.

———, Richard W. *War in the Persian Gulf: Operations DESERT SHIELD and DESERT STORM, August 1990-March 1991*. Washington, D.C.: Center of Military History, 2010.

———, Richard W. ed. *American Military History Volume II: The United States Army in a Global Era, 1917-2008*. Washington D.C.: Center of Military History, 2009.

———, Richard M. *"Lucky War:" Third Army in Desert Storm*. Fort Leavenworth, KS: U.S. Army Command and General Staff College Press, 1990.

Task Force Devil Combined Arms Assessment Team. *The Modern Warrior's Combat Load: Dismounted Operations in Afghanistan, April-May 2003*. Fort Leavenworth: Center for Army Lessons Learned, 2003.

Tifft, Susan, Johanna McGeary and Christopher Redman. "A Treasure Trove of Documents." *Time* 122, no. 21 (1983): 44.

Tiron, Roxana. "NATO Units in Kosovo Predict Mission Could Last a Decade." *NationalDefense Magazine.org,* March 2003. http://www.nationaldefensemagazine.org/archive/2003/March/Pages/NATO_Units3922.aspx (accessed March 19, 2013).

United Nations Security Council. "United Nations Security Council Resolution 1244, Kosovo." June 10, 1999. http://daccess-dds-ny.un.org/doc/UNDOC/GEN/N99/172/89/PDF/N9917289.pdf?OpenElement (accessed March 18, 1999).

United States. Presidential Commission on the Assignment of Women in the Armed Forces. *Report to the President*. Washington: The Commission, 1992.

United States. National Commission on Terrorist Attacks Upon the United States. *The 9/11 Commission Report*. Washington D.C.: Government Printing Office, 2004.

United States Department of the Army, Army Central Public Affairs. "Third Army now U.S. Army Central." U.S. Army Central. http://www.centcom.mil/news/third-army-now-u-s-army-central (accessed March 25, 2013).

United States Department of the Army. Army Doctrinal Reference Publication (ADRP) 3-0, *Unified Land Operations*. Washington D.C.: Headquarters, U.S. Department of the Army, May 2012.

———. Army Doctrinal Reference Publication (ADRP) 3-90, *Offense and Defense*. Washington, D.C.: Department of the Army, August 31, 2012.

———. Army Regulation 600-13, *Army Policy for the Assignment of Female Soldiers*. Washington, D.C.: U.S. Department of the Army, March 27, 1992.

———. Department of the Army Pamphlet 611-21, *Military Occupational Classification and Structure*. Washington, D.C.: U.S. Department of the Army, January 22, 2007.

———. Field Manual 3-0, *Operations*. Washington, D.C.: Headquarters, U.S. Department of the Army, June 2001.

———. Field Manual 5-19, *Composite Risk Management*. Washington, D.C.: U.S. Department of the Army, August 2006.

———. Field Manual 21-18, *Foot Marches*. Washington, D.C.: U.S. Department of the Army, 1990.

———. *Personnel Policy Guidance for Overseas Contingency Operations*. Washington D.C.: U.S. Department of the Army, 2009.

———. "Soldier's Creed." United States Department of the Army. www.army.mil/values/soldiers.html (accessed March 27, 2013).

United States Department of the Army Center for Army Lessons Learned. "Grenada Chronology." Working paper, n.d.

———. *OEF Initial Impressions Report*. Fort Leavenworth, KS: Center for Army Lessons Learned, December 2003.

United States Department of the Army Center of Military History. "Campaigns of the U.S. Army. United States Army Center for Military History. http://www.history.army.mil/html/reference/campaigns.html (accessed October 3, 2012).

United States Department of the Army Human Resources Command Awards and Decorations Branch. "Global War on Terrorism Expeditionary Medal GWOTEM and Global War on Terrorism Service Medal GWOTSM." U.S. Army Human Resources Command. https://www.hrc.army.mil/TAGD/Global%20War%20on%20Terrorism%20Expeditionary%20Medal%20GWOTEM%20and%20Global%20War%20on%20Terrorism%20Service%20Medal%20GWOTSM (accessed March 22, 2013).

United States Department of the Army Medical Materiel Agency. *Medical Equipment Set Combat Medic Support and Consumables Handbook: 6545-01-609-2699, UA 246C, LIN U65480.* Fort Detrick, MD: U.S. Army Medical Materiel Agency, January 2013.

United States Department of Defense Office of the Assistant Secretary of Defense (Public Affairs). "Department Opens More Military Positions to Women." Department of Defense press release. http://www.defense.gov/Releases/Release.aspx?ReleaseID=15051 (accessed January 28, 2013).

United States Department of Defense Advisory Committee on Women in the Services (DACOWITS). *2009 Report.* By Claudia J. Kennedy, Roberta L. Santiago, and Felipe Torres. Washington D.C.: U.S. Department of Defense, 2010.

United States Department of Defense. *Conduct of the Persian Gulf War.* Washington, D.C.: Government Printing Office, 1992.

———. Joint Publication 1, *Doctrine for the Armed Forces of the United States.* Washington, D.C.: U.S. Department of Defense, March 25, 2013.

———. Joint Publication 1-02, *Department of Defense Dictionary of Military and Associated Terms.* Washington, D.C.: U.S. Department of Defense, August 15, 2011.

———. *Report to Congress: Kosovo/Operation ALLIED FORCE After Action Report, 31 January, 2000.* Washington, D.C.: Government Printing Office, 2000.

United States Department of Defense Task Force on Women in the Military. *Report.* Washington D.C.: Department of Defense, 1988.

United States Department of State and Department of Defense. *Grenada: A Preliminary Report.* Washington, D.C.: Government Printing Office, 1983.

United States Department of Veterans Affairs. *American Prisoners of War (POWs) and Missing in Action (MIAs),* by Robert E. Klein, Michael R. Wells, and Janet M. Somers. Report to the Office of the Assistant Secretary for Policy and Planning. Washington, D.C., April 2006.

United States General Accounting Office. *Report to the Secretary of Defense: Women in the Military, Deployment in the Persian Gulf War,* by Foy D. Wicker, Marilyn Mauch, Beverly Ann Bendekgey, Kathleen M. Joyce, Julio Luna, and David Moser. Report to the Secretary of Defense. Washington D.C., July 1993.

United States Library of Congress. Congressional Research Service. *Kosovo: U.S. and Allied Military Operations* by Steve Bowman. Washington, D.C.: The Service, 2000.

———. *Kosovo Conflict Chronology: September 1998 – March 1999* by Julie Kim. Washington, D.C.: The Service, 1999.

———. *Troop Levels in the Afghan and Iraq Wars, FY2001-FY2012: Cost and Other Potential Issues* by Amy Belasco. Washington, D.C.: The Service, 2009.

————. *War in Afghanistan: Strategy, Military Operations, and Other Issues for Congress* by Steve Bowman and Catherine Dale. Washington, D.C.: The Service, 2009.

Wadle, Ryan D. "Objective Lexington: Cougar Company under Fire in the Ganjgal Valley." In *Vanguard of Valor: Small Unit Actions in Afghanistan*, edited by Donald P. Wright 179-198. Fort Leavenworth, KS: Combat Studies Institute Press, 2011.

Wallace, Terrence M. and Everett A. Johnson. "Positively Focused and Fully Engaged: Lessons from Task Force FALCON." *Joint Center for Lessons Learned Bulletin* 2, no. 2 (June 2000): 30-33.

Wentz, Larry. *Lessons from Kosovo: The KFOR Experience.* Washington D.C.: DOD Command and Control Research Program, 2002.

"What is a Loya Jirga?" *BBC News,* July 1, 2002. http://news.bbc.co.uk/2/hi/south_asia/1782079.stm (accessed March 22, 2013).

Wojack, Adam N. "Integrating Women Into the Infantry." *Military Review* 82 (November-December 2002): 67-74.

Wong, Wong, Thomas A. Kolditz, Raymond A. Millen, and Terrence M. Potter. "Why They Fight: Combat Motivation in War." Monograph, U.S. Army War College, 2003.

Wright, Donald P. *A Different Kind of War: The United States Army in Operation ENDURING FREEDOM, October 2001-September 2005.* Fort Leavenworth, KS: Combat Studies Institute Press, 2010.

Yates, Lawrence A. *The U.S. Military Intervention in Panama: Origins, Planning, and Crisis Management June 1987-December 1989.* Washington D.C.: Center of Military History, 2008.

Yetiv, Steve A. *Persian Gulf Crisis.* Westport, CT: Greenwood Press, 1997

www.ingramcontent.com/pod-product-compliance
Lightning Source LLC
Chambersburg PA
CBHW080320290526
45790CB00005B/2117